3 Loop Tours

Walking with Women
THROUGH CHICAGO HISTORY II

Jean S. Hunt

Bloomington, IN   Milton Keynes, UK

authorHOUSE®

AuthorHouse™
1663 Liberty Drive, Suite 200
Bloomington, IN 47403
www.authorhouse.com
Phone: 1-800-839-8640

AuthorHouse™ *UK Ltd.*
500 Avebury Boulevard
Central Milton Keynes, MK9 2BE
www.authorhouse.co.uk
Phone: 08001974150

© *2007 Jean S. Hunt. All rights reserved.*

No part of this book may be reproduced, stored in a retrieval system, or transmitted by any means without the written permission of the author.

First published by AuthorHouse 3/2/2007

ISBN: 987-1-4259-9626-0 (sc)

Edited by Mary S. Nolan
Cover Photo: Chicago History Museum
Book Design: Barbara Ciurej & Julie Africk
© *Chicago 2007*

Printed in the United States of America
Bloomington, Indiana

This book is printed on acid-free paper.

For
Amanda Ruth Medendorp
&
Grace Anne Medendorp

ACKNOWLEDGEMENTS

MY HEARTFELT THANKS TO MY FRIENDS AND COLLEAGUES IN THE Chicago Area Women's History Council (formerly Conference) for thirty-five years of adding to my knowledge of women's history and stimulating my classes and research.

Initiated and sponsored by the Chicago Area Women's History Council, in partnership with the Center for Women and Gender at the University of Illinois at Chicago, *Women Building Chicago 1790–1990: A Biographical Dictionary* is the indispensable reference book on the contributions of more than four hundred women to the history of Chicago. I am profoundly grateful to the editors and authors. *Women Building Chicago* is the backbone of this book and the first place to look for fully developed biographical information on many of the women cited here. In introducing a few of them, I hope you will be encouraged to go to *Women Building Chicago* for further reading and for bibliographic sources.

In a variety of different ways, Zoie Keithley, D Clancy, Mary Ann Johnson, Patricia Novick, Ellen Hunt, Sarah Hunt, and David Medendorp have served as prods, encouragers, and inspiration.

Lester Hunt has been considerate, supportive, thoughtful, and incredibly generous.

Mary Nolan has been editing me for fifty-plus years, and I am forever in her debt.

INTRODUCTION

THEY HAVE LEFT US AN INCREDIBLY RICH AND VARIED LEGACY. *Walking With Women Through Chicago History II* wants to take you around a very small portion of the city and introduce you to some of these fascinating women and tell you about some of their struggles and triumphs.

The walks are very short, but the text is longer than is usual in a guidebook. You may want to read some of it before you begin the walk, or you might just take advantage of the many places in the Loop where it's possible to sit down, both indoors and out. Perhaps you might even take some time simply to people-watch, and to consider that all those who contribute to history in their individual, unique ways come in a variety of shapes and sizes, fashionable and otherwise.

Sometimes we fail to appreciate what we have been given. Americans often ignore the profound importance of our inheritance from Native Americans, even though place names like Chicago or Illinois should remind us. Descendants of immigrants though we are, we forget how hard they worked to shape the built environment and, what's more, create an intellectual, social, and cultural world for us to enjoy. It is hard to move forward if we refuse to know our history and acknowledge our debts. Implicit in the legacy is a challenge.

Tour One

start: Michigan and Wacker
end: Michigan and Randolph
time: 1 hour with reading stops

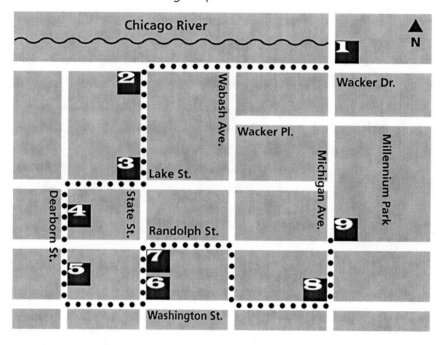

 Walk to the northeast corner of Michigan Avenue and Wacker Drive and then take a few steps to the east and stand facing the river.

This is a very good place to think about the phenomenal growth of a tiny settlement into a great city and the crucial role that women played—from the very beginning—in the history of Chicago.

From the Atlantic Ocean into Canada's St. Lawrence River and then to the Great Lakes, the French explorers and *voyageurs* came into the heart of the country. They paddled westward down the Chicago River and then carried their canoes above their heads through a short and muddy overland trek, a *portage*. This brought them to the Des Plaines River, which soon flowed into the Illinois River and then into the mighty Mississippi.

For centuries, Native Americans had used this route. The first Europeans to do so were Louis Joliet and a group of *voyageurs* that he had recruited in Montreal, Canada, and whom he provisioned and paid. That exploration in 1673 included a Jesuit priest as well, Pere Jacques Marquette.

An estimated 100,000 Native Americans lived in the Great Lakes area at that time. The tribe that dominated the Chicago area was the Potawatomi. There were a few small villages hugging the banks of the Chicago River near its outlet to Lake Michigan, with dome-shaped wigwams that were designed and built by women to shelter their families. Each year in the fall, these villages disbanded, and the families moved to separate hunting locations in nearby forests.

1756-1809? CATHERINE DU SABLE

As you look across the river, you will see the tall, bronze Equitable Insurance Company building and next to it the five-story Gleacher Center, the downtown campus of the University of Chicago. A little more than a hundred years after the Joliet-Marquette expedition, a very prosperous fur-trading post was built on that site. A multiracial, multicultural family named du Sable settled there and started Chicago on its path to great commercial success and world renown.

Jean Baptiste Point du Sable, of French and African-Caribbean descent, had married a Potawatomi woman in a ceremony "according to the custom of the country"; later he married her in a Catholic ceremony. Her Native American name is unknown; **Catherine** was the name recorded on her marriage certificate.

Marriage to Catherine was advantageous for Jean Baptiste. Traders lived in what has been described as a climate of peril and loneliness. One thing that they could do to lighten their boredom and save their skins was to make a "country marriage." Like European royalty, Native Americans used

> Like European royalty, Native Americans used marriage to assure the stability of their alliances.

3

A view of Chicago in 1779 (then called Eschikago) with Catherine's home and a painting of Jean Baptiste Point du Sable.

••••••••••••

SIDE TRIP

A **Chicago Tribute** marker honoring **Catherine and Jean Baptiste Point du Sable** *is located across the bridge, on the east side of Michigan Avenue between Tribune Tower and the Equitable Building. The space between the buildings is called Pioneer Court.*

Some eighty Tribute markers have been erected throughout Chicago, and a map and brief biographies of the honorees are available at the Chicago Cultural Center, where this tour will end. Of the eighty persons so honored, twenty-nine are Chicago women.

marriage as the principal way to assure the stability of intertribal and trading alliances. And the Potawatomi tribe, important as middlemen in the fur trade, was famous for doing so.

Being the wife of a fur trader had many benefits and offered Catherine an alternative to the difficult life of an Indian woman. It certainly provided a more reliable food supply and was richer in material comforts. It may have been physically easier, although most of what we know about Indian women in this period of history is through the eyes of men of another race and another culture. They often described Native American women as drudges.

Catherine's workload would have included cooking, cleaning, child care, and laundry, as well as gardening, netting snowshoes, preparing hides, and making and decorating moccasins, clothing, belts, cradle boards, and baskets. She would have welcomed European technology, trading for goods such as cooking pots, beads, blankets, and cloth, because they would lighten her daily tasks.

The du Sable post was a huge success because it was a working partnership. Catherine played key economic and political roles. After all, it was her kinsmen and clan connections which were the essential foundation of the business. Moreover, Catherine had an even more important function, from history's point of view: she was a cultural broker, a go-between, often helping one community understand the practices and beliefs of the other. Fur-trading societies worked because each side gave and took, and Indian wives of the traders were among the most important intermediaries.

To understand early American history, certainly early Chicago history, it is essential to understand the fur trade and its consequences. Each group of European settlers who came to this continent had to figure out how to establish an economic base. They had to have something to sell or exchange in order to obtain the food, clothing, and tools they needed to survive in a harsh new environment. Exploiting the natural resources of their new home was the most logical first step.

An often-precarious existence could be had from fishing, hunting, gathering, and perhaps growing some crops. For some time the fur trade was merely a sideline, but then demand surged when tall beaver hats for men became a craze in the cities of Europe. A man of fashion in London or Paris would often purchase an extra seat at the opera just for his hat. (A side note: making these "felted" hats involved a process that required the use of mercury. The chemical fumes destroyed the brain cells of the workers, which in turn spawned the phrase "mad as a hatter.") Thus the fad in men's headgear on one continent changed the course of history on this one.

The Potawatomi were major players in Great Lakes trade. Like other Native American groups, they understood that they were making and accepting changes in relationships, alliances, and lifestyles. What they did not foresee, perhaps, was that they were exchanging self-sufficiency for technological dependency. Guns, iron kettles, ammunition, and blankets all became essential to the Native Americans and were available only through continued trade with the French Canadians or other Europeans.

1781?–1840 ARCHANGE OUILMETTE

Looking north across the river, you will see a tall, white structure, the Wrigley Building, on the west side of Michigan Avenue. More than two hundred years ago this was the site of the Ouilmette homestead. Antoine Ouilmette came to the area in 1790 with his wife, **Archange**. She was a woman of "mixed blood," a *métis*; her mother was a Potawatomi, her father a white fur trader. The Ouilmettes had eight children who grew to maturity, four girls and four boys.

Native American families were usually small, with two or three children the norm. There were many sexual taboos, and periods of abstinence were common. Still, Indian couples seemed to do as well or better than modern married couples in terms of frequency of intercourse. Children were welcomed, and childlessness was the chief reason for the dissolution of a marriage. In such cases, the bride price was given back to the husband, and the marriage was over. Abortion was practiced; as

> The Ouilmette family represents the people "in between," the term often given to families of mixed race, religion, and culture.

far as is known, Native Americans did not think it a crime. Survival issues may best explain the small family size. Even in an area rich in wildlife, both fish and fowl, as well as in berries and nuts, a lack of food was a persistent problem, and women and children were the first to feel its effects.

On the other hand, the attitudes and practices of French Canadian and other whites, especially those who were Catholic, made large families of eight to twelve or more children quite common. Archange's family of eight was more typical of the new "mixed blood" families than was the du Sable family with two children. Indian mothers usually nursed their children for two or three years, a custom which Archange may have followed, since the births of her children were spaced over thirty years.

While the du Sables may be said to be the founders of a modern American city, the Ouilmette family is an important part of the Chicago story as well, for they represent the people "in between," as families of mixed race, religion, and culture often were called. It is likely that Ouilmette migrated to the Chicago area because of the 1763 treaty ending the French and Indian War (the American phase of the Seven Years' War in Europe, also called the Great War for Empire). The war's aftermath caused significant changes in the fur trade.

The French had to cede Canada to the British, and thus the English and Scotch increasingly controlled the fur trade in Canada. French Canadians were demoted to the bottom of the heap and found it impossible to climb back up. So Antoine Ouilmette migrated to Chicago, but in the year that he arrived the last buffalo hunt was held in this area, and horses were quickly becoming more important than canoes in the fur-trading business. Although he started out as a trader, Antoine was later known as a man who raised horses and other animals.

In 1801, the du Sables sold their post. The inventory of the sale tells us that they had a large house with other structures: bake house, smokehouse, poultry house, and barn. They owned two mules, thirty head of cattle, thirty-eight hogs, and four hens, very impressive for a frontier establishment. Perhaps even more impressive were the household furnishings, which included a cabinet of French walnut with four glass doors, a couch, candlesticks, mirrors, and even two pictures. The du Sables had arrived in the 1780s, less than twenty years earlier, but despite the relative shortness of their time in the area, they left a lasting legacy.

In contrast, the Ouilmettes remained for almost fifty years. As a part-Potawatomi, Archange would have followed many native customs and traditions in the daily life of her household. Indians in this area usually ate two meals each day, in mid-morning and evening. Fur trading seemed to stimulate the appetite: reports told of a family with an extra man or two putting away thirty or forty rabbits a day or numerous whitefish of four to six pounds each.

Like Catherine du Sable, Archange would have had the woman's role of growing all the crops, such as melons, squash, beans, and corn. She may have planted and harvested a little tobacco, too. In addition, their table would have had wild nuts, berries, and edible wild plants. Surplus fish would be smoked or dried. Meat from large animals could also be smoked or made into pemmican, a paste of dried and pounded meat.

Early spring was a time for tapping maple trees and making sugar, a very important seasoning in most Indian meals. Sugaring-off was a joyful, gala time, when women and children went out together into the woods to set the great kettles boiling. If snow was still on the ground, they might use their long paddles to throw some of the boiling liquid on the snow, making instant candy for the children.

The Americans

The Treaty of Paris, signed in 1787 after the American Revolution, caused another change in the fur trade and, indeed, in the frontier itself. The treaty gave the fledgling country of the United States sovereignty over "the West," an immense territory that stretched from the Appalachian Mountains to the Mississippi River.

The new "owners" did not immediately have the resources to control the vast and unsettled Northwest Territory, but, even so, the terms of the treaty were not good news to Native Americans and others involved in the fur trade. The Indians preferred to deal with the British, who acted as if the treaty had not been written and continued to trade as before. Political and military alliances were readily created between British and Indians, because the British interests lay only in the fur trade. The new Americans intended to settle permanently and own their land, which threatened the livelihood of the Indians. Besides, the concept of ownership was contrary to Native American life and value systems.

Because an American presence in the new territory was necessary in order to validate the claim to the area, President Thomas Jefferson ordered that a fort be built on the Chicago River. If you turn around and look down while standing at the bridge, you will see the shape or "footprint" of that fort outlined in brass embedded in the sidewalk and roadway of Michigan Avenue.

ca 1780-1841? ANN BISHOP WHISTLER

With her eight surviving children and a daughter-in-law, Ann took shelter in a miserable hut while soldiers built Fort Dearborn.

In the summer of 1803, fifty-six soldiers marched out of Detroit to the site of the new Fort Dearborn. Their commander, Captain John Whistler, came by schooner, together with his wife, **Ann**, their family, and all the heavy equipment. In a memoir many years later, Julia Fearson Whistler, the young wife of Ann's and John's oldest son, William, who was a lieutenant under his father's command, described the scene of their arrival. About two thousand Indians watched the ship, she wrote; they thought it was a huge canoe with wings.

When the troops arrived, they found four log cabins straggling along the river's bank. One was the vacated du Sable post, which had been purchased by Jean La Lime, who would become the interpreter at Fort Dearborn. A second was the Ouilmette home, while two other French/Indian families, headed by Pierre Le May and Louis Pettle, occupied the other two cabins.

The ground the fort was to be built on was about eight feet higher than any of the surrounding land. As the soldiers built the fort, which John Whistler had designed, they were handicapped by a lack of tools as well as inadequate food and clothing. While it was going up, Ann and her family took temporary shelter in what Julia described as a wretched, bark-covered hut. The soldiers camped in the open.

Ann had given birth to fifteen children, but only four daughters and four sons survived. When they arrived at what was to be Chicago, these children ranged in age from three to twenty-year-old William. Together with Ann's daughter-in-law, Julia, they came to know the rigors and monotony of a fort that was almost as isolated as if it had been on another planet. Fresh supplies of staples like tea, flour, sugar, and tobacco, as well as tools, uniforms, and clothing, did not arrive until a year later, in the summer of 1804.

Trading at Fort Dearborn

The family was poor—John's pay was $40 per month—and they were frequently in debt. Once John wrote a creditor that he had had no pay at all for two years. While at Chicago he was almost arrested for non-payment of some debts, and it took him two years to clear the record. Not only was he underpaid; the job of commander was far from easy. Standards for admission into the army were not high, and about a third of the men in Whistler's command were foreigners; many were illiterate. Excessive drinking was a common problem, despite the punishment of twenty-five to a hundred lashes and sometimes reduction in rank.

When Fort Dearborn was finally built, Ann had the luxury of a cramped two-room apartment. Living under such conditions was unhealthy for everyone: after a year, Whistler wrote to his superiors that half of his men had been ill. In July 1805 he reported that Ann was at the point of death, in constant pain, and that frequent bloodletting was the only thing that offered her any relief. The fort had a doctor, but it is unlikely that he would have known very much about the folk medicine of the Indians, which might have been helpful. Moreover, the white women who increasingly began to appear on the frontier seldom sought the advice of the Native American women who were there before them.

There were happy times, of course: beautiful weather, the welcome company of a traveler, the excitement of a horse race, and family celebrations. In 1804, the Whistlers' eldest daughter, Sarah, married, the first wedding to take place at the fort. A year later, Ann's first grandson was born to Julia and William.

The Whistler family also figured in a later period, connected with what is often considered America's most famous painting, *Whistler's Mother, A Study in Grey and White*. Ann was the paternal grandmother of the painter, James McNeill Whistler, who was the son of George Washington Whistler, that three-year-old child at the time the family arrived in Chicago.

Within a short time after Fort Dearborn was erected, some soldiers married or brought their wives to live at the fort. If life was cramped for the Whistler women, for the wife of a common soldier it was much more burdensome, and she would have had little or no privacy. There were no separate quarters; she would eat and sleep in the barracks among the rank-and-file troops. She took on work, if she could; washerwoman for officers and other soldiers was a likely occupation. Or she might work for military and other government officials, such as doctors or Indian agents, who lived near the fort and came to own horses and other animals. Dr. John Cooper, the second surgeon at the fort, employed the wife of a soldier to milk his cows and make butter, and her husband earned a little extra money by taking care of Cooper's two horses.

1770–1840? ELEANOR LYTLE MCKILLOP KINZIE

Next to purchase the du Sable post was John Kinzie (originally MacKinzie). He arrived at the small settlement in 1804 with his wife Eleanor and their son, John Harris Kinzie, and bought the post from Jean La Lime.

Eleanor Lytle McKillop was the widow of an army officer when she met and married John Kinzie. Like John's first wife, Eleanor had been an Indian captive. Her daughter-in-law, Juliette Magill Kinzie, recounted the story in her book *Wau-Bun*. She wrote of it just as Eleanor had told it to her, she said.

In the fall of 1779, the Lytle family lived near Fort Pitt (now Pittsburgh). Eleanor, nicknamed Nelly, was nine. Preparing for winter, some trees had been cut down, and logs and big branches were lying around the cabin waiting to be turned into firewood. Nelly and her seven-year-old brother were playing there when they thought they saw a Native American man peering through the branches. They ran to tell their mother, who did not take them seriously. She was tired of all the false alarms and tales she heard from neighbors; in her experience, the Indians who frequented the area and visited their cabin were both friendly and pleasant.

The children returned to their play and were sitting on one of the tree trunks when they were seized from behind, cautioned to silence on pain of death, and led away. Their captors were Seneca Indians who had hoped to wreak havoc on their enemies, the Delaware tribe, a group that traded with the fort and the people in the area. Disappointed when their original plan failed, the Senecas took the Lytle children as a consolation prize.

Another small task force from the marauding group later returned to the cabin and captured Mrs. Lytle herself and her three-month-old infant. Two other small children, four and six years of age, hid in a raspberry patch, and a servant girl crawled into a large brewing tub in the outer kitchen. These three were not discovered and thus were spared the long march to the Seneca village.

The children returned to their play and were sitting on one of the tree trunks when they were seized from behind, cautioned to silence on pain of death, and led away. Their captors were Seneca Indians.

Mr. Lytle had gone with his farmhand to help raise a barn, and he returned home to an ominous quiet. He ran to neighbors to see if they knew what had happened; when he could find no answers, a search party was organized. Searching through the night, the party was unable to find Lytle's wife and children. When morning came, the discouraged men went to Fort Pitt to ask the help of the commander and the Indian agent.

On the march, the terrified and weary mother and her two oldest children were befriended by a kindly man who seemed to be the leader of the group. When they finally rested for the night, he shared his food with them, and his solicitude gave Mrs. Lytle hope that they might simply be held for ransom. As they renewed their trek the next morning, another man offered to carry the baby. His steps got slower and slower; after he had fallen well behind the group, he killed the baby by crushing its head against a tree. When he reappeared, Mrs. Lytle realized what had happened, but in fear for the safety of her other children she made no protest.

In her memoir, Juliette Kinzie calls the one who befriended the Lytle family "Big White Man." Some historians have argued that his anglicized name was Corn Planter. Whatever his name, he "adopted" Eleanor. It was a custom among many Native Americans that the chief mourner of a beloved child, spouse, or other relative might adopt a substitute as soon as possible after the death. Big White Man presented Nelly to his mother, who had lost a son the year before in a battle with the Lenape tribe, and he arranged to take Eleanor with him to his lodge to live with his family as his sister. He arranged for Mrs. Lytle and her

Eleanor's experience underscores how important the knowledge of Native American culture, customs, language, and relationships was as a qualification for a white woman marrying a fur trader.

son to stay under the care of his mother until such time as they could be ransomed.

This had happened during the Revolutionary War, when the Seneca, Iroquois, and other tribal members of the Five Nations were British allies and implacable in their hostility to the Americans. Delicate negotiations were required to allow Mr. Lytle and his rescue party into the Seneca village. It was easy to arrange for the release of Mrs. Lytle and their son, but no amount of trade goods or other offers, promises, or pleas could secure the deliverance of Eleanor. Big White Man's new sister was dear to him, a substitute for his dead brother, and nothing could induce him to part with her. Eleanor's frustrated and heartsick parents had to return home without her.

Nelly was loved and treated well by everyone except Big White Man's wife, an allegedly difficult woman who had no children of her own. She seemed to look for opportunities to hurt Nelly or to make her uncomfortable, even going so far as to try to poison the little girl with liquid concocted from the root of the May apple, the strongest poison known among Native Americans. Warned by another member of the tribe, Eleanor refused to drink the brew, and her attacker was derided and suffered semi-banishment, left to hoe in the most distant fields.

Eleanor loved her new family, although she sorely missed her own kin. There were more than three hundred different tribal languages in America, and she became fluent in the Seneca language and perhaps had knowledge of others. Then the end of the Revolutionary War precipitated a realignment of relationships with many tribes, including the Senecas. It also gave hope to Mr. and Mrs. Lytle that now they might be able to reopen negotiations with Big White Man.

The Lytles sent an emissary, who arrived at the time of the Feast of the Green Corn, a gala occasion. Juliette wrote in *Wau-Bun* that thirteen-year-old Eleanor was dressed in

> . . . a petticoat of blue broadcloth, an upper garment of black silk, ornamented with three rows of silver brooches, the center ones from the throat to the hem

being of large size and those from the shoulder down being no larger than a shilling piece and set as closely as possible. Leggings of scarlet cloth and moccasins of deer skin embroidered with porcupine quills completed her costume.

The emissary's wrenching stories of the efforts of Nelly's parents and their grief softened the heart of Big White Man. He agreed to bring his "sister" to the Grand Council at Fort Niagara, on the British (i.e., Canadian) side of the Niagara River, provided that he heard no more pleas and that there would be no effort to take the child from him. Supported by all the officers from Fort Pitt and especially by their wives, the Lytles waited impatiently for the first sight of the Seneca delegation.

Nelly had promised that she would not leave Big White Man without his permission. Boats were sent to ferry the Senecas across the river to the American side. Although there was ample transportation for all the members of the Seneca delegation and their horses, Big White Man asked them to wait on the Canadian side. He held Nelly's hand as they crossed the river, but as soon as the boat landed and Nelly saw her mother, she flew into her arms.

In retelling the story many years later, Eleanor recalled that Big White Man said, "She shall go. The mother must have her child again. I will go back alone." No arguments or entreaties would persuade him to remain at the Council. He re-crossed the river and disappeared into the forest with all the young men who had come to the meeting with him.

The Lytles did not leave Fort Niagara for several weeks, afraid that there might be some effort to recapture Eleanor. Nothing happened, but their constant worry caused them to move across Lake Erie to Detroit, Michigan, where a year later, at fourteen, Eleanor met and married McKillop.

She never saw her Indian "brother" again, but for the rest of her life she remembered him, his mother, and her life among the Seneca tribe with great affection. This experience of Eleanor's, like that of Kinzie's first wife, Margaret, who had been a captive of the Shawnees, was a great asset, and it underscores the importance that the knowledge of Native American culture, customs, language, and relationships had as a qualification for a white woman marrying a fur trader.

The Whistlers were at Fort Dearborn until 1810 and, as a conscientious officer, John Whistler tried to enforce government regulations regarding the supply of liquor to Native Americans. But John Kinzie, the principal trader in the area, found these rules impossible to obey if his business was to be a success. Quarrels of this sort between traders and the military were common in frontier posts, but this one festered. Eventually, every officer at the fort had taken sides. Charges were brought against the officers, but the War Department was unable to assemble a court that could fairly sit in judgment. Consequently, it was decided to reassign Whistler to Detroit, considered at that time a hardship post because it was a much more expensive place to live. The other officers were scattered to different posts all over the country.

ca 1780-1846? REBEKAH WELLS HEALD

Succeeding Whistler as commander of Fort Dearborn was Captain Nathan Heald, the son of an army officer who had joined the army at an early age. He was thirty-six when he married **Rebekah Wells** in 1811. She was a niece of Captain Billy Wells, a part-Miami Indian who worked as an Indian scout; Heald met her while visiting Fort Wayne in Indiana. Immediately after their wedding, the Healds started on the rigorous trip to Chicago, sleeping under the stars if the weather allowed and enduring the conditions of wilderness travel. Accompanying Rebekah was her slave, Cicely.

The Northwest Ordinance of 1787, written immediately after the new territory was acquired following the Revolutionary War, proclaimed that "involuntary servitude," save in punishment for crime, was prohibited. Despite this clear injunction, slavery was not unknown in the Northwest Territory, nor in the new town of Chicago. Captain Heald himself owned two male servants while at Fort Dearborn. Jefferson Davis, serving in the Army Corps of Engineers, had a personal slave during all of his years of service in the "Old Northwest." John Kinzie and his half-brother, Thomas Forsythe, who together owned a trading post in Peoria, purchased an African-American named Jeffery Nash at Detroit in 1803. They made a contract under which Nash was to be a seven-year indentured servant. The supposed contract aside, he was actually held and treated like a slave. He escaped from Peoria to New Orleans, causing Kinzie and Forsythe to sue to have their property returned to them. The suit was tried in the Supreme Court of Louisiana, and the court ruled against them, on the grounds that slavery was outlawed in the territory where they lived.

When the War of 1812 began, the majority of the new white

settlers in the Northwest Territory welcomed this second war with the British, for they blamed them for the insecurity of the frontier. Most native tribes continued to be loyal to the British, even as they traded with the Americans. For their part, the settlers were full of resentment against the British and thought that the war would solve the "Indian problem." Some even entertained the idea of making Canada a part of the United States.

> When the War of 1812 began, the Chicago community outside the fort consisted of four or five families like the Ouilmettes: French Canadian men with Native American wives.

Despite its distance and isolation from Washington and London, the Northwest Territory was, ironically, the area of the country in the greatest danger during the war. It was so thinly settled by Americans that its villages were spread out and exposed. After the United States Congress declared war on June 18, it was not long before those who had settled around the Great Lakes tasted battle.

In less than a month, on July 17, the British had captured Mackinac Island. At Fort Dearborn, Captain Heald was ordered by his superiors to abandon the fort and march to Fort Wayne. John Kinzie urged Heald and others to leave immediately or else stay inside the security of the fort, where there was a six-months' supply of ammunition and food. But Heald maintained that his orders required him to distribute the fort's supplies to the local Potawatomi Indians. Although these orders were received on August 7, Heald did not order the abandonment of the fort until August 15.

The Chicago community outside the fort then consisted of four or five families like the Ouilmettes: French Canadian men with Native American wives. They did not go with the garrison on its march to Fort Wayne, since marriage meant full membership in the tribe, and kinship exempted them from any harm. However, having been warned of restlessness and a possible attack, John Kinzie put all the members of his own family into canoes, with two Native American friends guarding them. Kinzie's family was at the mouth of the river, at what is now Madison Street, when the assault began.

The contingent from the fort was proceeding along the sandy, scrub-brush lakefront and had reached what is now 18th Street and Prairie Avenue when a group of Indian warriors attacked them. Heald had added fifteen white males from the area to the military complement of fifty-five, inducting them into the army; however, three left before the march. Captain Billy Wells had come from Fort Wayne with a small group of Miami warriors to help protect his niece, Rebekah Heald. They were on horseback, as were Rebekah and several officers from the fort, followed by the marching soldiers and, at the end, several wagons carrying eighteen children and nine women, all of whom were in some way attached to present or former members of the Dearborn garrison. This number included the slave, Cicely, and her child. The twelve village inductees and John Kinzie, who had marched out with them, protected the wagons.

When the attack came, Billy Wells was the first casualty. All twelve inductees were immediately killed, although Kinzie was not. The Miami who had accompanied Captain Wells were riding along the fringes, and they melted away. The wagons, meant to be a protection for the women and children, turned out to be traps, preventing the occupants from trying to scatter and run. Only six of the children in the wagons survived, and two of the nine women were killed, one of whom was Cicely with her baby. John Kinzie had once tried to buy her, offering $600. This offer was remembered forty years later when, as an old woman, Mrs. Heald filed papers to get compensation for the loss she suffered when Cicely and her infant son were killed in 1812. Her request was never granted.

Out of ninety-two evacuees, forty-two survived the battle on the lakefront. In addition to the six children, there were twenty-nine soldiers and seven women, but eight of these survivors died in captivity. Two years later, nine Fort Dearborn soldiers were taken from Quebec and distributed among the Indians as servants, where they remained for nine more months before a fur trader named Robert Dickson ransomed them. After his release, one of these men, James Corben, was discharged from the army as unfit for further service. He had no money to get from New York to his home in Virginia, so rather than face starvation, he tried

Rebekah Heald was on horseback during the attack and was wounded twelve times. She was held for ransom until a fur trader paid a mule and a bottle of whiskey to purchase her freedom.

to reenlist. For a few years thereafter he received a small pension, but in 1820 he was taken off the list. The army argued that Indians killed their wounded prisoners and, since Corben was alive, he could not have been wounded in the Chicago battle. Six years later, upon reconsideration, the government awarded him a pension of $4 a month.

Rebekah Heald, who was on horseback during the attack, was wounded twelve times but survived. She and Captain Heald, who was also wounded, were helped to safety but held for ransom by Indians friendly to the Kinzie family. A fur trader paid a mule and a bottle of whiskey to purchase Rebekah's freedom.

Another woman who survived the Fort Dearborn massacre was Margaret McKillop Helm, the wife of a lieutenant posted at Fort Dearborn and a daughter of Eleanor Kinzie and her first husband. An Indian called Black Partridge, another Kinzie friend, took her to the Ouilmette's cabin. There she was hidden under a quilt by Archange and her sister. They sat on the quilt, with Margaret underneath, when the raiding Indians came back to look for anyone who might have escaped and to destroy the fort.

A statue commemorating Margaret Helm's rescue by Black Partridge stood for many years at the battle site at 18th Street and Prairie Avenue, some two miles south of the river. Owned by the City of Chicago, it was more recently displayed in the entrance hall of the Chicago History Museum, as the former Chicago Historical Society is now known. Perhaps the statue will again be on view now that the renovation is completed.

A New Era

Fort Dearborn was rebuilt in 1816, and the Ouilmettes and a few other *métis* families formed the nucleus of a new settlement on the ruins of the devastated village, but the fur trade had begun a precipitous decline. Then in 1829, the Treaty of Prairie du Chien awarded Archange and her children clear title to two sections of land on the north shore of Lake Michigan, in what is now the suburb named for them, Wilmette. The family moved that year, and farming, especially raising animals, became their chief occupation. A visitor wrote that they occupied a large block house good enough for a congressman to live in; that they owned horses, cattle, wagons, and a carriage; and that the children were said to be very comely, well dressed, and intelligent.

A steady trickle of American settlers from New England and upper New York State migrated to the greener grass of the Midwest, changing the culture and composition of the growing frontier town on the lake. In 1830, Chicago's population totaled one hundred, a multiracial, multicultural mix of Potawatomi, French Canadians, a few African-Americans, the soldiers garrisoned at the fort, their families, and other American settlers. By the end of the decade, more than four thousand people resided here.

Indeed, Chicago was so packed with newcomers—Yankee settlers, businessmen, laborers who came to work on the Illinois & Michigan Canal, speculators, sailors, and those just passing through—that it was impossible to shelter all of them. If licensing had been in effect, half of the dwellings in town would have been classified as boarding houses. Families often lived in their covered wagons until some sort of housing could be built. In 1835, only twenty per cent of the population had been here longer than a year.

Bowing to the increasing pressure of the new migrants, the government signed a treaty in 1837 which provided for the removal of all Potawatomi Indians to west of the Mississippi River. Some fled to Wisconsin or Canada, but the vast majority, including Archange Ouilmette and her family, began the long trek to a reservation in Kansas. Fort Dearborn was a viable presence until 1840, after which it gradually deteriorated and was finally demolished in 1856.

From where you are standing at Michigan and Wacker, walk a few yards to see the four Michigan Avenue bridge-tenders' houses, with sculptures on each of them.

The southeast one, called *Regeneration*, depicts the rebuilding of the city immediately after the Great Fire of 1871. The symbolic figure of a woman represents the "I Will" spirit of Chicago's people. Cross Michigan Avenue to see the sculpture on the southwest corner of the bridge, *Defense*, a memorial to the August 1812 Fort Dearborn Massacre. The sculptors, respectively, were James Earle Fraser, who had studied at the School of the Art Institute of Chicago, and Henry Hering; they were completed in 1928.

Regeneration, *Michigan Avenue*

SIDE TRIP

Two more sculptures are on the north side of the bridge. On the northwest corner, **The Discoverers** *commemorates the Joliet and Marquette expedition that arrived here in 1673. On the northeast side,* **The Pioneers** *honors John Kinzie, who purchased the du Sable cabin. The woman on horseback, carrying her infant, suggests the pioneering migrants who braved wilderness routes to populate Chicago.*

As you walk west along the river, away from Michigan Avenue, you might think of the river's many uses. In the 1800s it often froze in the winter, allowing the soldiers at the fort to ice-skate on it and even use it for horse races. An early Methodist minister used the river for baptisms. The river was Chicago's first port: imagine it teeming with masts, as hundreds of ships came all the way from the Atlantic Ocean, by way of Canada's

St. Lawrence River and the Great Lakes, to dock here. Chicago received 440,000 tons of goods by ship in 1844, increasing astronomically to more than three million tons by 1869. In any twelve-hour period, a ship might pass under the drawbridges every two minutes. The greatest number of arrivals in a single day totaled three hundred ships.

Of course, this increase in commerce meant pollution, augmented by increasing domestic sewage and industrial waste. The McCormick Reaper Works, for example, was located on the north side of the river near where the gleaming white Wrigley Building now stands. "The Works" was one of the largest manufacturing plants in the Midwest.

1835?-1923 NETTIE FOWLER McCORMICK

Nancy Maria "Nettie" Fowler McCormick was the mother of seven children and a prominent figure socially. Surprisingly, she was also heavily involved in "The Works." When the great fire of 1871 destroyed the factory, Nettie persuaded her husband, Cyrus, twenty-six years older than she, not only to rebuild but also to modernize.

Often caught between the prevailing Christian and Victorian ideals of womanliness and motherhood on one hand and her own talents on the other, Nettie effectively ran the business for several years before Cyrus's death in 1884, and she certainly did so for many years afterward. In 1902 she helped to put together the merger of McCormick with several other firms, including the John Deere Company, into a new entity called International Harvester.

Today the river sees water taxis and tour boats, motor and sailboats, barges, canoes, racing shells, and even the occasional gondola. Now and then a tall ship will moor along the banks, but it is hard to visualize swimmers. In 1892 a massive project was begun, designed to reverse the flow of the river away from the lake to prevent the polluted water from contaminating the growing community's water supply. Typhoid fever, amoebic dysentery, and cholera were all well-known "visitors" to Chicagoans. The project to create the new twenty-eight-mile-long Chicago Sanitary and Ship Canal involved cutting through a ridge of glacial moraine and bedrock to the west; it was the largest single earth-moving project in the history of public works to that time. The canal was completed in 1906 and the water flow was reversed, forever.

1903-1927 SYBIL BAUER

The river was cleaner in 1921 when *The Chicago Journal*, one of the city's many daily newspapers, sponsored a Chicago River Marathon. Not yet eighteen years old and a mere high school student, **Sybil Bauer** astonished everyone with her victory in the contest. Most people thought that it was unseemly for a woman to be in competitive sports at all, but this young woman was so exceptional that she became the first woman to surpass male swimming records—which led to a debate about whether she should be allowed to compete against men. The final decision was a resounding "No."

Sybil went on to break all standing records for women's backstroke. She held twenty-three world records and won "Gold" in the 1924 Olympics in Paris. She accomplished all of this despite the fact that she was allowed to practice only when male swimmers did not need the pool, and she had to make do with the poorest accommodations.

In 1926, as she was looking forward to her marriage to Ed Sullivan, a sportswriter in New York, Sybil was diagnosed as having intestinal cancer, and she died that year. Her fiancé later hosted a television variety show, "The Ed Sullivan Show," probably best remembered for introducing the English musical quartet, the Beatles, to United States audiences.

Continue walking along the river to State Street at Wacker Drive.

In 1954 a plaque was placed on the southwest corner to indicate the site of a school and commemorate the work of its founder, Eliza Chappell, but new construction is a menace to historical markers, and the plaque has disappeared.

1807-1888 ELIZA CHAPPELL PORTER

Remembered as Chicago's first public school teacher, **Eliza Chappell** arrived in Chicago in 1833 and opened a school that received some of its financing from the public school fund. Parents and children were anxious for education, and enrollment grew rapidly. Eliza provided boarding facilities so that the school could take girls from the farms nearby, who would otherwise have had no access to schooling.

This success came at a high price, however. Frail and sickly all her life, Eliza became ill and had to give up her teaching duties. When she recovered, she married a missionary, Jeremiah Porter, who established Chicago's first Presbyterian church. For a short time they lived in a log cabin where snow filtered through the cracks onto the quilt on their bed, and wolves howled along the banks of the river further interrupting sleep.

Remembered as Chicago's first public school teacher, Eliza Chappell was also a Civil War nurse.

As missionaries, the Porter family moved to several other communities in the Midwest, returning to Chicago in 1858. In the intervening years, Eliza had given birth to nine children, three of whom died in infancy. Two other children died of typhus shortly after the family returned to the city.

During the Civil War years of 1861–1865, Eliza plunged into sanitary commission work, assisting groups that collected and distributed supplies to soldiers at the battlefront. (See Tour II for more about the Northwest Sanitary Commission, in the sections about Dr. Mary Harris Thompson and especially Mary Livermore and Jane Hoge.) Eliza also served as a nurse in rudimentary hospitals, both in the battlefield and in towns close to military action. She and her husband were instrumental in persuading President Abraham Lincoln to send wounded soldiers back north or to their homes so that they could receive better medical care.

The Porter family moved around a good deal, and Eliza often started schools wherever she had an opportunity. After the Emancipation Proclamation of 1863, for example, she started a school for freed slaves in Memphis, Tennessee.

 From State and Wacker, walk one block south to Lake Street and turn west for one block under the famous—at one time infamous—Lake Street "el."

> While the first elevated train lines were built in New York in 1870, in Chicago the first line began operation in June 1892. The bribes and huge payoffs to city aldermen to guarantee its operation quickly became known. Unfortunately, such corruption was commonplace.

In the 1820s, 1830s, and 1840s, it was Lake Street that was "that great street" (as State ultimately became known). Chicago was a frontier town, and the number of men far exceeded the number of women. The riverfront was the center of activity as well as the source of most jobs, and the majority of these workingmen lived in boarding houses on Lake Street, a short walk from the wharves and warehouses. A British visitor in 1820, Charles Joseph Latrobe, described one Chicago hotel as "filthy, vile, and noisy," and it is likely that many of the boarding houses also met those standards. Scattered among them, of course, were houses of ill repute as well as taverns.

 At Dearborn, turn left and walk south toward Randolph Street.

The Heart of the Theater District

Across Dearborn you will see the facades of two now-defunct theaters, the Harris and the Selwyn. The splendidly renovated spaces are now part of the new home of the Goodman Theater, which actually extends behind the original facades of the old theaters. (The first site of the Goodman was at Monroe Street and Columbus Avenue, behind the Art Institute. A new extension of the Art Institute is replacing it.)

As you walk south from Lake Street on the east side of Dearborn, you will find a metal-framed sign at the edge of the sidewalk that gives a brief history of these two theaters and lists some of the stars, such as Audrey Hepburn and Tallulah Bankhead, who performed there.

Dearborn and Randolph streets have been the heart of professional theater in Chicago for more than 170 years. The first professional show opened in 1834 (twenty-five cents for children, fifty cents for adults). Three years later, the rich tradition of resident theater companies was inaugurated. The season was usually six weeks long, with the playbill changing nightly, after which the company went on tour. Conversely, traveling shows and companies, usually from New York, visited Chicago on a regular basis. In 1847, John B. Rice built the first theater building near the corner of Dearborn and Randolph. Ten years later, the McVickers Theater was erected. By 1920, there were twenty-three legitimate theaters in Chicago, seating hundreds of theatergoers. The Harris and the Selwyn, as well as the Fine Arts theater on South Michigan Avenue (see Tour III), were the smallest of them all.

1873-1955 CHARLOTTE BARROWS CHORPENNING

For twenty years Charlotte gave children a chance to act in plays and see productions.

The original Kenneth Sawyer Goodman Memorial Theater opened in 1922 and is Chicago's oldest not-for-profit theater. Plays at the Goodman, which had a drama school for those who wanted to pursue a professional career in theater, were of very high quality. For many years it had a beloved and well attended Children's Theater, and **Charlotte Chorpenning** was its director. From the 1930s into the 1950s, she led a movement to give children the opportunity to act in plays and especially to see theater productions. Charlotte wrote many new plays or dramatized well-known children's stories to expand the repertory for children. The Children's Theater Press (now Anchorage Press) published 943 scripts written for children, and Charlotte had written 188 of them.

1902-1987 HELEN TIEKEN GERAGHTY

One of the students at the Goodman School of Drama was **Helen Tieken**. She was not interested in acting but rather in directing and producing, especially outdoor spectacles and large-scale productions. Her first work was with the Junior League, putting together a touring National Children's Theater. Shortly afterwards, she produced Maurice Maeterlinck's *Blue Bird*, and her production toured fifteen cities.

In 1933, Chicago hosted its second world's fair, A Century of Progress, celebrating one hundred years since the incorporation of the village of Chicago. (Incorporation as a city occurred four years later, in 1837.) Helen happily produced large-scale historical dramas presented at the fair. One of these, *Wings of the Century*, involved 150 professional actors and props that included thirteen trains, horses, boats, and a model of the Wright brothers' airplane. A thousand people saw the production each day.

The Great Depression and World War II were not good times for pageants. Helen Geraghty went on to direct the Actors Guild at Hull House and taught at Francis Parker School. Then in 1948, the railroad industry wanted to put on an extravaganza in Chicago to celebrate one hundred years of railroad history. Helen produced *Wheels A-Rolling*, which followed the pattern she had set for her productions at the Century of Progress, using professionals and, in this case, trains and other pieces of railroad equipment. In 1949 she produced a similar show; in 1950 she researched and wrote a large historical pageant. Newspaper reporters who interviewed her were invariably surprised by her small stature, given the huge and complex productions she produced.

Industrial shows, dramatic histories of corporations for trade conventions, and special events for fundraisers all kept Helen busy. These projects required long hours, and she often gave her children small parts in her productions so as not to be away from her family. She traveled widely to find talent for the shows that were part of the trade fairs sponsored by the Chicago Association of Commerce and Industry from 1957 to 1963 at Navy Pier.

1900-1987 IRENE SEATON WICKER

A student at the Goodman Theater School for three years, **Irene Seaton** married Walter Wicker, and they carved out successful careers in radio during its "golden age" in the 1930s and 1940s.

(A side note: Walter's grandfather and great uncle had owned land just northwest of downtown Chicago which they donated to the city. The name of Wicker Park is also the name given to the neighborhood that surrounds the park.)

> With few available actors, radio programs required enormous versatility. Irene sometimes played twenty-seven different roles in a single show.

In 1929 and 1930 Irene appeared in several of the Goodman's professional productions. She became the star of a radio show for children in 1930, the only one that won the PTA's full approval. Irene's show was a combination of singing and storytelling; for forty years she was known as "the Singing Lady."

Programming for the show was unique and varied. Children's classics like *Alice in Wonderland* and *Jack in the Beanstalk* were offered, as was a series of biographies of great artists, such as Mozart, Rubens, and Verdi. Irene interviewed famous persons, among them Franklin D. Roosevelt and "America's Sweetheart," movie star Mary Pickford, and they told the stories of their own childhoods to those listening.

All of this was hard work. Irene Wicker researched and wrote scripts that were barely completed before the actors went on the air. There were few actors available, so radio programs required enormous versatility. Irene sometimes played as many as twenty-seven different roles during a single show. Often, at the close of her show she would run to another studio and transform herself into Hedda Gabler or Anna Christie, or play Greta in a drama based on the life of Greta Garbo.

By 1936 Irene was the highest-paid woman in radio. She also played a part in the development of television. In many early TV presentations, actors had to crawl from the stage in order to stay out of range of the stationary cameras. "The Maker of Dreams," presented in 1931, was the first television drama in the Midwest to be synchronized with radio.

Famous for wholesome children's entertainment for more than twenty years, Irene's radio show was immediately cancelled in 1950 when a private blacklist accused her, along with Dorothy Parker, Leonard Bernstein, and Arthur Miller, among others, of being Communist sympathizers. Despite the fact that the charges could not be proved, her show stayed off the air for two years; when it returned it was unable to recapture as large an audience. Still, although the show was less popular than before, Irene Wicker won both Emmy and Peabody awards in the 1960s.

 As you walk south on Dearborn to Washington, you will see a large city block (formerly known as Block 37) where construction began in 2006.

1887-1978 SYLVIA SHAW JUDSON HASKINS

Remaining in the middle of the site along Dearborn is a small Art Deco building built in 1931 for Commonwealth Edison and now landmarked. If you look above the entrance, you will see a sculpture by **Sylvia Shaw Judson**.

Sylvia's first studio was the laundry room in the basement of the apartment building she moved into shortly after her marriage to Clay Judson. Sculpture is often bold, impressive, and monumental, but Judson's work is quiet, delicate, and restrained. Locally, her best known works are the *Girl with the Violin* and *Dancer*, both in Ravinia Park north of the city; the Stations of the Cross in the Church of the Sacred Heart in Winnetka; and a large fountain at Brookfield Zoo.

Outside the Chicago area, *Bird Girl*, in a Savannah, Georgia cemetery, was photographed for the cover of John Berendt's novel, *Midnight in the Garden of Good and Evil*, and was also seen in the movie of the same name. Visitors to Boston are likely to remember the monument to Mary Dyer in front of the Massachusetts State House facing the Boston Common, where Dyer died a Quaker martyr. Copies of this statue are at Earlham College in Richmond, Indiana, and in Friends Center in Philadelphia. The Dyer monument is one of only a handful of statues in the United States commemorating a real woman.

Looking to your right along Dearborn, you will see the city's municipal courthouse, the Daley Center. Near the Washington Street side there is a great steel sculpture given to the city by Pablo Picasso. This abstract head of a woman, made of corrosive tensile (Cor-Ten) steel, the same material as the building behind it, often wears wreaths or hats in season, so that she can participate in various city celebrations.

Continue walking south to Washington Street and turn east one block to the northeast corner of State and Washington.

On the corner of the building above your head is the famous Marshall Field's clock. Beneath this clock and its twin at State and Randolph, generations of Chicagoans have arranged to meet friends. In 2006 Federated Stores bought Field's and renamed it Macy's, despite an outpouring of negative public sentiment from Chicagoans whose families had shopped in this building for more than a hundred years.

SIDE TRIP

Entering Field's/Macy's at State and Washington, walk to the center of this large space and you will find yourself under a very handsome blue mosaic dome many floors up. It was designed and built by the Louis Comfort Tiffany Company. For a closer look at the intricate work, you can go up to a balcony on the fifth floor.

Creating Careers

As you see, the twelve-story Marshall Field/Macy building covers an entire block. Built in 1902, the store's famous slogan was "Give the lady what she wants." Department stores were a new concept then, giving women an opportunity to shop for everything they wanted under one roof, rather than in many small, specialized stores. They also provided new employment opportunities for women. Field's had more than eight thousand employees in 1904, some of them women creating innovative new careers for themselves, like the three women on the next pages.

1857-1932 HARRIET CONVERSE TILDEN BRAINARD MOODY

Now known as one of the original financial backers of *Poetry* magazine and a great patron of the arts in Chicago, **Harriet Converse Tilden** had entered into a disastrous marriage to a Chicago lawyer, Edwin Brainard, in 1876. Divorced in the 1880s, she soon had to assume the care and support of her invalid mother after her father died. She became a teacher but quickly discovered that her salary was insufficient to cover household costs.

Harriet's solution was to sell gingerbread to Marshall Field's, followed a short time later by chicken salad. From the basement of her home she developed a catering operation and helped to stock the dining cars of many railroads, as well as the larders of clubs, corporations, and tearooms. She supported herself this way until her business failed in 1929, when she was seventy-two.

But she added another kind of spice to the city as an ardent supporter of struggling poets, writers, musicians, and painters. Her Michigan Avenue restaurant, Le Petit Gourmet, was the setting for frequent poetry readings. Each member of the audience contributed one dollar, and the evening's poet received all the money collected. Harriet also organized poetry readings at the University of Chicago and at Northwestern University. Widowed in 1910 after a brief second marriage to William Vaughn Moody, a professor of English and a poet, Harriet Moody became known for her salons and unforgettable dinner parties. Guests stayed into the wee small hours; along with great food they got memorable and witty conversation.

1870-1952 ANNA J. MURPHY PETERSON

Another woman who left a bad marriage was **Anna Peterson**, who came to Chicago as a "widow" and supported herself at Field's. She began by demonstrating toys but soon was capturing audiences with her knowledge of cooking and household techniques. Gas and electricity became common in city homes in the 1920s, and new stoves, refrigerators, washing machines, irons, and hot water heaters were changing the work and the routines of American housewives.

Peoples Gas Company decided to open a Home Service Department in 1922, and Anna Peterson became its first director. In a modern kitchen she gave cooking classes for PG employees, and later she opened the classes to the public. The first broadcasts on those new-fangled radios began in 1924, and so did Anna Peterson. Her popular fifteen-minute program was subsequently printed in the *Chicago Evening Standard*, complete with recipes.

Anna stressed the importance of vegetables and told her listeners about things they had not heard of before, such as vitamins. During the long, harsh depression years of the 1930s, Anna responded with classes on canning food and sewing. She worked out economical meal plans and helped women to figure out ways to stretch their meager budgets.

1900-1952 FRITZI SCHERMER BROD

A recognized textile designer at home in Prague, she brought patterns in the modern style to Field's conservative customers.

Born in Prague, **Fritzi Schermer** met the man who was to become her husband when he was traveling in Europe buying books for Brentano's, a New York bookstore. On his return to the United States, he was asked to become the head of the Art Department in Kroch's and Brentano's bookstore in Chicago. Although the city seemed to resist modern art, Oswald Brod made sure that Chicagoans had access to all the latest books on the subject. He also made them available at discount prices to the small local community of contemporary artists. When Frizi married Oswald in 1924, she immediately became part of this vibrant group.

A recognized textile designer at home in Prague, in Chicago she became one of the first to bring her patterns, very much in the modern style, to conservative customers at Field's. She did some design and painting work for the Balaban & Katz movie palaces as well, but she was very serious about art and soon began to take classes in painting and lithography. A *Chicago Tribune* art critic was one of the few who recognized her talent and wrote positive reviews of her exhibits.

Fritzi began to get much more public recognition and appreciation of her work in the early 1950s, when modernism became widely acceptable. Although not a fan of modern painting, a *Chicago Daily News* art critic told readers that a Fritzi Brod exhibit was just too good to miss. Ill with cancer, Fritzi died in 1952.

1880-1944 RUTH HANNA MCCORMICK

A lecture given in the tearoom of Field's helped to make **Ruth McCormick** a political activist. Both she and her husband, Joseph Medill McCormick, had lived and worked at the University of Chicago Settlement House under assumed names. This experience, plus Joseph's 1910 lecture, convinced Ruth that women must become involved in political activity. She organized a committee of ten women who worked with the Women's Trade Union League, an organization that vigorously supported minimum wage and other labor legislation. Ruth also used her network and organizing talents to get both a Children's Bureau and a Women's Bureau established under the United States Department of Labor.

In 1912, pregnant with her first child, Ruth was elected to the Illinois House of Representatives. Eight years later, she was the first woman to serve on the executive committee of the Republican National Committee. Although she was not reelected in 1930, she was a woman who had many other interests. After her husband died in 1925, Ruth supervised her large farm, owned a Rockford, Illinois, newspaper, and also owned a radio station.

Walk north one block on State Street (or go through the store, which covers the block) to the southeast corner of Randolph and State, under the other clock. This was the site of the long-gone Central Music Hall.

1853-1916 CATHARINE GOGGIN *AND*
1861-1937 MARGARET ANGELA HALEY

Choose: get married or teach. For many years, those were the only options open to young women. **Catharine Goggin** chose to teach. After doing so for twenty years, she drew up a list of problems confronting Chicago teachers that might be remedied by better management and practices. No one listened. In 1897, Goggin organized a meeting of ten women teachers at the Central Music Hall.

31

It was the beginning of the Chicago Teachers Federation. The new organization was for elementary teachers only, almost all of whom were women. At that time, administrators and high school teachers tended to be men.

More than half of the five thousand eligible teachers joined the Federation. They had plenty of grievances, especially inadequate pay: they had not had an increase in salary in twenty years. Sometimes they were forced to take a pay decrease during the school year, when the school board said it was too poor. The board argued for the right of children to an education and used that argument to deny teachers *their* rights.

Goggin was elected the first president of the union but served for only two years. She did not like being in the spotlight, but she continued to work diligently for teachers as secretary of the union until her death in 1916. Her friend **Margaret Haley** became the president and public voice of the Chicago Teachers Federation from 1901 to 1939. In Margaret's autobiography, she wrote about her "forty fighting years."

A major battle was over the issue of teacher autonomy vs. enlightened administration; the latter translated into rule from the top down. William Rainey Harper, founder and head of the University of Chicago, was appointed to lead a commission to study school problems. It reported that university-trained administrators should decide what went on in classrooms, a concept that dominated Chicago schools for more than thirty years.

In 1915 the school board passed the Loeb Rule, stating that teachers were forbidden to join labor unions. Thirty-eight teachers refused to resign from the Federation and were immediately fired. The Illinois Supreme Court upheld the Loeb Rule, but the following year a teacher tenure bill passed the Illinois State legislature, and the teachers were reinstated.

During the Great Depression, Haley's fights were over "payless paydays" and the requirement that teachers take loyalty oaths. Pay scales that were based on gender and grade level clearly discriminated against grade school teachers.

In 1937 the Chicago Teachers Federation was absorbed into the Chicago Teachers Union.

From State and Randolph, walk east on Randolph one block to Wabash Avenue and then south one block to Washington. Turn east again on Washington and walk one more block to the corner of Michigan Avenue. On the northwest corner is the Chicago Cultural Center.

1831-1894 MYRA COLBY BRADWELL

Pause for a moment to look across the street to the south, to the large office building at 30 North Michigan. **Myra Bradwell's** home was here, the place where, in 1869, she began to publish the *Chicago Legal News*. For a quarter of a century, Myra discussed the work of other lawyers, pending legislation, and reform issues in her publication. She had twice been denied admission to the bar, initially on the grounds that she was a married woman and later simply on the grounds that she was a woman. In 1890, the Illinois Supreme Court reversed its decision and admitted her to the bar; she was fifty-nine years of age.

There were one or two prominent legal publications on the east coast, but Myra Bradwell's *News* was the most important legal newsletter in the Midwest. She used it to press for reform legislation with regard to railroads, local zoning, temperance, prison reform, and especially the rights of women. An 1861 Illinois law gave a woman the right to own property, but it was under the control of her husband. A new law in 1869 gave a woman the right to transfer, contract, and use her property as she saw fit. This law also stipulated that in all cases a widow was to receive an interest in her husband's property.

Myra became more and more interested in suffrage. As a moderate, she worked with Lucy Stone and Mary Livermore. In 1893, after Illinois women got limited suffrage allowing them to vote in local elections, she cast her first vote in a Chicago School Board election.

SIDE TRIP

Now walk into the Cultural Center, a treasure house of the work of Tiffany and other artists. As you go in the Washington Street entrance, you will encounter an incredible display of Tiffany mosaics. These continue up to the third floor, opening into Preston Bradley Hall, where the ceiling boasts the largest Tiffany dome in the world. Leave the room on the far side, go down the ramp to the second floor, and turn right to find a second Tiffany dome in the Grand Army of the Republic Hall.

Free tours of the building are given weekly; details can be found at the information desks in either the Washington or Randolph Street lobby. Near the Randolph Street end is a Chicago Tourism Center, which has monthly schedules of the various art exhibits as well as frequent lectures and daily free concerts. The Tourism Center also has the Chicago Tribute maps mentioned earlier, plus information on public transportation, theater offerings, cultural institutions and programs, and a variety of architecture and neighborhood tours, some by river boat.

1905-1995 GERTRUDE E. GSCHEIDLE

This wonderful 1897 treasure house now known as the Cultural Center was actually built to house the Chicago Public Library. After the fire in 1871, Queen Victoria—and many British citizens—donated some eight thousand books to the devastated city. These were originally housed in an empty water tower and became the core of the public library collection.

Many women worked in this building, helping patrons find books, searching reference sources, reading to children, initiating and helping to build special collections. Fifty-three years after the library's founding, a woman became chief librarian for the first time. She was **Gertrude Gscheidle**, and she served as chief librarian from 1950 to 1967.

1907-2003 ELEANOR "SIS" GUILFOYLE DALEY

In the late twentieth century, the library in this proud Beaux Arts building found that it had to keep up with new library technology. Along with plans to build a new, modern facility there was talk of tearing down the "old" building. In one of the first and most important fights to preserve Chicago's heritage, **Eleanor "Sis" Daley**, the wife of then Mayor Richard J. Daley (and the mother of Mayor Richard M. Daley), led the fight to save the building. Having kept a low profile in the midst of tumultuous political times, Sis Daley was respected and admired by many Chicagoans as an ideal Catholic wife and mother. Usually she was silent in the public arena; when she did use her voice, she was listened to and supported. This cause was one of those times.

1899-1996 CLAUDIA CASSIDY

On the second floor on the Randolph Street side of the Cultural Center is a five-hundred-seat theater named after **Claudia Cassidy**, the influential theater and performing arts critic who worked for several Chicago newspapers before signing on at the *Chicago Tribune* in 1942. After 1965, in addition to contributing freelance articles to the *Tribune*, she began to write for *Chicago Magazine* and to do a weekly broadcast on the local fine arts station, WFMT.

A significant number of harsh critiques earned Claudia the nickname "Acidy Cassidy," but she also praised and promoted the careers of Maria Callas, Carol Channing, and Tennessee Williams, among others. She was a stalwart supporter of the Lyric Opera; her last published piece was an article for the Lyric's program book for the 1990-1991 season.

Controversial, critical, and most often right, Claudia engaged Chicagoans for a quarter of a century. They wanted to know what Claudia had to say.

SIDE TRIP

Exit the Cultural Center at the Randolph Street end, cross Michigan, and walk east on Randolph about a half-block to the Joan W. and Irving R. Harris Theater for Music and Dance. When it was built in 2003 there were rigorous codes about buildings and building heights in the park, and so the plans for this theater turned the structure upside down: the balcony is at street level and the orchestra level is several stories below—at twenty-five feet below the level of the lake. The orchestra pit is forty feet below the lake.

Hanging from the ceiling at the street-level entrance is a large backdrop made of wood. Originally designed for a production of **Orfeo ed Euridice** presented by the Opera Theatre of Saint Louis, this challenging, stunning work by New York sculptor Louise Nevelson significantly enhances the minimalist design of the theater's lobby. (Another reference to a Nevelson sculpture follows the discussion of Lucy Page in Tour II.)

If you go into the Harris Theater, you will see a gleaming stage curtain designed by a local textile artist, Maya Romanoff. The sheer curtain has colored metal threads hand-woven into it so that it will reflect the stage lights.

You might want to stroll through Millennium Park at this point. Just behind the Harris Theater is the Pritzker Pavilion, designed by Frank Gehry. A huge sculpture, **Cloud Gate**, by Anish Kapoor is to the west; locals have nicknamed it "the Bean." And there is Jaume Plensa's Crown Fountain. The giant screens in each brick tower flash photographs taken of a thousand different Chicagoans from every walk of life. The shots, filmed by students of the School of the Art Institute, appear one at a time on the tall towers. At the south end of the park is the Lurie Garden, designed by landscape architect Kathryn Gustafson, who also designed the Diana, Princess of Wales Memorial in London.

Making History Now

The woman in charge of this vast domain, **Lois Weisberg,** *is Chicago's Commissioner of Cultural Affairs. She has turned a preserved building into a vibrant and enriching venue. The Cultural Center is truly a palace for Chicago's people, and program events are designed for everyone—adults, children, those who live in the city or just visit, people from every walk of life. With few exceptions, the hundreds of concerts, exhibitions, ethnic festivals, dances, and plays are free.*

While you are in the park or at the corner of Michigan and Randolph, stand for a few minutes to look north, south, and east. Everything you see east of Michigan Avenue is built on landfill.

Downtown lakefront in 1858 showing Michigan Avenue entrance to the Illinois Central depot, with the tracks and rail yards in the background.

A Municipal Solution

In early Chicago, the waters of Lake Michigan lapped up onto the street, making it muddy and causing erosion and loud laments from the landowners and residents of the elaborate houses that lined the west side of Michigan Avenue (until they were swept away by the Great Chicago Fire of 1871). The city could not afford to build a breakwater, but they did find an interesting solution: they let a railroad build its tracks out in the lake. In 1851, Chicago solved its lakefront problem and created an eyesore that lasted a century and a half.

The age of railroads had already begun in Chicago in 1848. When a second-hand locomotive puffed into town, it represented the first real challenge to the supremacy of the ribbons of rivers and canals that were the first transportation highways. Shortly thereafter, a new company, the Illinois Central Railroad, needed a terminal in Chicago. With a raft of political and financial backers, they proposed to build a breakwater if they could have a terminal on the river.

The alternative way to finance such a project would, of course, be through increasing taxes. A citizens' lobby against any tax increase won the day, and the Illinois Central immediately began work on a stone masonry breakwater between Randolph and 22d streets. Between the new breakwall and the old shoreline along Michigan Avenue, a lagoon formed. At first, this could be pleasant: children skated on it during the winter or played along the water in the summer.

The tracks were built on a trestle out in the lake, and in 1856 the first train, a wood-burning locomotive with two cars, puffed into the new station. A working station still exists under the Prudential and Aon buildings on the north side of Randolph Street; the Illinois Central sold the air rights above its station. The tracks, which carry southbound commuters, remained in the open until the building of Millennium Park in 2004 and can still be seen farther south at Monroe Street. There they run between the main building of the Art Institute on one side and the former Goodman Theater and the School of the Art Institute on the other. When a new annex of the Art Institute opens in Spring 2009, it will replace the former Goodman and be built over the tracks. There are no plans as yet to cover the tracks that are visible south of Jackson Boulevard.

The new lakefront created by the railroad quickly became thoroughly industrialized. Tracks fanned out to enter a huge railroad shed. Two gigantic grain elevators became the "skyscrapers" of the city, standing defiantly on the north bank of the river. Packing houses and grain dryers, plus a few storefronts and Lake House, Chicago's busiest hotel, completed the picture. South of Monroe, what was supposed to be a park was a mess. There were wharves, piles of boards, rocks, garbage, a wooden sidewalk, and a dirt beach. And the situation did not improve much over the next few decades.

Michigan Avenue in 1871

Filling in the Lakefront

Everything you see around you is part of the legacy of the Chicago fire of 1871. Between July and October that year, less than an inch of rain fell, and in the first week of October more than thirty fires were put out. Much of the city was built of pinewood, and construction was flimsy. In poor neighborhoods, thousands of rickety shanties crowded hard upon each other.

On October 8, a hot, windy Sunday evening, another fire started in the stable behind a wooden house belonging to Patrick and Catherine O'Leary at what was then 137 DeKoven Street; it is now the site of the Chicago Fire Academy, at 558 West DeKoven Street. Rumor had it that Mrs. O'Leary's cow kicked over a lantern in the barn and set the hay on fire, a story that persisted until it was held as fact. Catherine O'Leary denied it to her dying day. A more plausible explanation is that a man boarding in a neighbor's house had a bit too much to drink, went to the barn to sleep it off, and caused the fire. Ironically, neither the stable itself nor the O'Leary's house burned down in the fierce blaze that followed.

A delay in reporting the fire, plus more delays, confusion, and downright inefficiency, hampered the volunteer fire companies. Meanwhile, thirty-mile-an-hour winds sent flames leaping from one wooden structure to another. The path of destruction included the entire Loop and went north to Fullerton Avenue (2400 North). Thousands ran to the "blessed" lakeshore. Enterprising men with wagons, coaches, or carts offered rides away from the fire for $150.

Eighteen thousand homes, stores, bridges, railroad stations, factories, and churches were reduced to rubble. Two hundred and fifty people were known to be dead, and as many or more were never accounted for. Property damage totaled $200 million; in today's money it would represent a Bill Gates fortune. The debris from the fire was swept into the lake, and acres and acres of this landfill gave Chicago a new front yard. The destruction of virtually every building of importance was a clarion call to architects. Chicago would be rebuilt by the best.

Grant Park and even Millennium Park of 2004 can be said to be legacies of the fire. The lakefront area has seen many events over the years, like an international aviation meet in 1911 witnessed by three to four million people. The performing pilots were paid $2 for every minute they were in the air, which encouraged them to take their planes up often and stay as long as possible. The sky above the park was continually dotted with small planes.

As you look over at the Pritzker Pavilion, the band shell with its soaring silver grace notes, you are reminded that the park has played a major role in the musical life of thousands of Chicagoans. In addition to modern day blues, jazz, Gospel, and salsa festivals, there have been free concerts of classical music every summer for more than seventy years.

1907-1988 ANNE RUDOLPH

Those who have used the lakefront have come in all shapes and sizes. One was **Anne Rudolph**, who had an international reputation as a dancer and had performed at the Goodman Theater as well as at the Civic Theater. She was interested in the science of movement and in 1934 opened the Anne Rudolph School of Modern Body Education and Dance, where she worked with infants with handicaps and people with spinal problems. Just as happens in the park today, Anne held classes in Grant Park, encouraging passersby to join in. Fees were minimal, and she never refused a student who could not pay.

1896-1963 # EBBA SUNDSTROM

In its beginnings in Chicago, the classical music world was not very welcoming to women who wished to play its repertoire. Symphony orchestras did not allow women members, and there was a dearth of opportunities for women musicians to perform. To remedy this, violinist **Ebba Sundstrom** co-founded the Women's Symphony Orchestra of Chicago (WSOC). She worked with Richard Czerwonky, her teacher, and Marion Ochsner to bring together highly trained and talented women. The new orchestra played many standard works in order to prove themselves, but they also introduced audiences to the work of Chicago women composers, such as Carrie Jacobs Bond, Florence Price, and Eleanor Freer.

She was the first U.S. woman to be a permanent conductor of a professional orchestra.

Czerwonky conducted the orchestra, since no women were adequately trained, but for the 1928-1929 season at the 8th Street Theater, Ebba conducted, and she received great reviews. She was thus the first woman in the United States to be a permanent conductor of a professional orchestra, a position she went on to hold for eight years. The WSOC performed at Grant Park music festivals and at the 1933 Chicago World's Fair, and the orchestra also toured. It became known across the country through radio broadcasts on national networks.

The WSOC differed from other orchestras composed of women in that all its players were paid, and most were members of the musicians' union. During the 1937-1938 season, however, a deficit of $3,500 was discovered. Many embarrassing questions were asked, and under this pressure Ebba Sundstrom took a leave of absence and did not return.

1902-1976 GLADYS WELGE

The assistant conductor of the WSOC for eight years had been **Gladys Welge**, and she replaced Ebba Sundstrom as conductor. Gladys had opened her own school of music in her family home when she was only seventeen years old. She taught violin and her brother taught piano. Her school grew to fourteen teachers who used every inch of space available in the house. Gladys's first conducting experience was with an orchestra composed of the school's students, which gave frequent recitals at the school as well as an annual concert in downtown Chicago.

As an outstanding violinist, Gladys was one of the first to be admitted to the Women's Symphony Orchestra of Chicago. Like other women musicians, she had never even been permitted to audition for any major orchestra. This began to change during the Second World War, 1941–1945, when orchestras could not find enough men and began to accept women into formerly all-male ensembles. The Women's Symphony Orchestra of Chicago played its last concerts in 1945.

> At seventeen she had her own music school in her home.

This is the end of Tour I.

Tour Two

start: Washington and Dearborn
end: Monroe and Michigan
time: 1 hour with reading stops

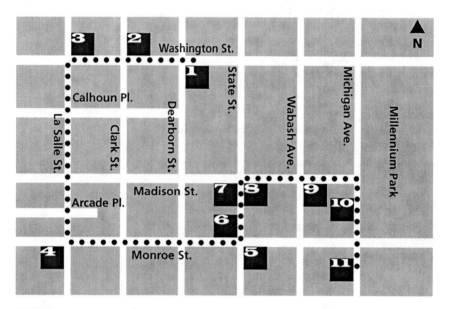

1 Begin this tour at Brunswick Plaza, just east of the Chicago Temple at the southeast corner of Washington and Dearborn streets.

In this courtyard is a sculpture by the Barcelona-born Spanish artist Joan Miró, titled *Miró's Chicago*. Installed in 1981, the thirty-nine-foot-tall piece suggests a nurturing mother. On the west side of the plaza is a series of stained glass windows embedded in the wall of the Chicago Temple building that depict the history of the First United Methodist Church; the fourth window shows Augustus Garrett and his wife.

The Chicago Temple building at 77 West Washington houses the First United Methodist Church on the first floor. You might want to cross the street so that you can look up to see the tall church steeple that caps the building. Immediately under the steeple is a small chapel with magnificent views of the city; it is often used for weddings.

1805-1855 ELIZA CLARK GARRETT

"Go west, young man." New York newspaper editor Horace Greeley's advice rang as loudly in the ears of young married couples seeking a better life as it did for young men. **Eliza Garrett** and her husband, Augustus, moved from New York State to Cincinnati, then to New Orleans, to escape from debts and the people who wanted them paid.

Finally, in 1834, they came to Chicago, and in that year Augustus sold real estate valued at almost $2 million. The business of land speculation—boom and bust—is an often neglected part of frontier settlement history. In Chicago's expanding community of four hundred persons, the Garretts became leaders. By 1856, the year after Eliza died, Chicago's population had grown to eighty-six thousand.

Eliza Garrett was a staunch member of the Clark Street Methodist Episcopal Church, now the First United Methodist Church. After her husband died in 1848, she used sixty percent of her annual income for charity and was especially concerned about education. Many clergymen in "the West," including the pastor of her own church, were poorly educated and badly trained. A very vocal group surprisingly justified this, arguing that too much education could lead to a corrupt clergy.

Eliza became the first woman to finance a biblical institute, and it was the first theological seminary outside of Vermont for the training of Methodist ministers. Her bequest also provided for room, board, and books for the students. She wanted the school to be away from the terrible evils of the city, so it was built in Evanston and remains today as part of the Northwestern University campus. Eliza's benefaction was an expansion of the role of women in churches.

Eliza and her husband engaged in the boom and bust of land speculation, an often neglected but crucial part of the history of expanding frontier settlements.

1888?–1977 MATILDA FENBERG

> A member of the first law school class at Yale to admit women, Matilda was proud that she never lost a jury trial.

Another, different connection with the Chicago Temple building is that of **Matilda Fenberg**. Born in Poland, Matilda grew up in Findlay, Ohio, where an incident in fourth grade set her on her path as a lawyer. One day a policeman came to take her from school to the courthouse to interpret for someone from her neighborhood who was accused of stealing. Matilda could speak Yiddish, German, and English, the only person in the area with those language skills. In the courtroom, the young girl defended her neighbor with such passion and vigor that the district attorney predicted that she would grow up to be another Clarence Darrow.

The new University of Chicago recruited Matilda, offering free tuition. But she could not afford food or rent or books, so she taught school for two years, saving every penny. After finally beginning classes, she tutored others in order to make ends meet. Despite the fact that her mother did not approve of educating girls, Matilda persisted, and she taught in small towns in Ohio to put her three sisters through college so that they could have teaching careers.

Matilda was a member of the first law school class at Yale University to admit women; she then practiced in her hometown. On a trip to Chicago, she determined that she had to meet her hero, Clarence Darrow, and she burst into his office in the Chicago Temple building unannounced. Nevertheless, he graciously invited her to sit down for a talk, and when she left she had an offer to come and work with him.

Matilda Fenberg was especially proud of the fact that throughout her career she never lost a jury trial. Women could not then serve on juries, and Matilda lobbied for ten years, beginning in 1929, to get legislation passed in Illinois that would allow women to serve. She also campaigned vigorously for the Equal Rights Amendment and was an early advocate of no-fault divorce.

1890-1975 PEARL HART

West from the Chicago Temple Building, on the southwest corner of Washington and Dearborn streets in 1912, stood the John Marshall Law School. Since college was not a requirement for admission, **Pearl Hart** entered immediately after finishing high school. From the earliest days of her career, she was dedicated to court reform and social and civil rights.

Illinois took a lead in court reform when the first Juvenile Court was established in 1899. A Morals Court, begun in 1913 (later called Women's Court), dealt with such issues as child abuse and abandonment, bastardy, and women criminals, usually prostitutes. Judges and the police often ignored the constitutional rights of women, and Pearl worked with other women lawyers, Hull House staff and residents, and members of women's clubs to bring about reform and better treatment.

Segregation in public schools, credit laws that hurt minorities, and the discrimination suffered by homosexuals were among her crusades.

In 1937 Pearl was one of the founders of the National Lawyers Guild (NLG). Most of the world was plunged into the Great Depression, which meant not only economic hard times but also political extremism. Fascism was rampant in parts of Europe and racism in the United States. The NLG members became defenders of civil rights and advocates for immigrants and trade unions, and Pearl continued to work for the rights of foreign-born residents well into the 1960s. Raids and deportation hearings of immigrants swelled to more than ten thousand in the years following World War II, feeding on concerns about national security and Communism.

In the postwar period, the public became increasingly aware of police raids, entrapment, and other injustices. More than three thousand people were dismissed from government posts or discharged from the armed services. Pearl Hart was a founding member of the Chicago Committee to Defend the Bill of Rights, set up to address such injustice. Segregation in Chicago's public schools and credit laws that discriminated against minorities were among her many crusades, as was the discrimination suffered by homosexuals. She spent the last decade of her life working to gain recognition of gay and lesbian civil rights.

From Dearborn, walk west on Washington one block to Clark Street.

On your left across the street, you will see the Daley Center, with the great steel sculpture by Pablo Picasso (see also Tour I). Made of the same structural material as the building it adorns, the sculpture was installed in 1967, the first monumental modern sculpture to be placed in the downtown area.

On the Clark Street side of Daley Plaza is a site associated with the woman discussed below.

1829-1895 MARY HARRIS THOMPSON

In 1860 when **Mary Harris Thompson** wanted to become a doctor, women were simply not admitted to recognized medical colleges. She enrolled in the New England Female Medical College and also spent a year getting clinical experience at the New York Infirmary for Women and Children. After completing her degree in 1863, she moved to Chicago. She did not want to compete with other women doctors for patients, and Chicago was a growing community where there was a great need for doctors.

Mary began her work in Chicago with the United States Sanitary Commission, a civilian group that had worked throughout the Civil War to aid the medical department of the Union army. The Commission addressed various needs, among them adequate funds to buy needed medical supplies; a better system for distributing supplies; and improving the ability of the medical department to keep up with the demands for treatment and nursing of the wounded and dying. Mary Livermore and Jane Hoge managed the Chicago branch of the Commission. (See below for Livermore and Hoge.)

After the war, many veterans came with their families to Chicago, and many of them lived in dire poverty. Dr. Thompson realized that there was a critical need for a hospital for women and children, and in 1865 she opened the Chicago Hospital for Women and Children. More than seven hundred people poured into the new facility the first year, with five hundred seeking free treatment in the outpatient dispensary and the balance of two hundred admitted to the hospital at a cost of five dollars per week. Only one inpatient was able to pay the full amount; the other 199 paid whatever they could afford.

Still, Mary knew that her education and training were inadequate, since women's medical colleges were not able to provide the faculty, staff, labs, and other facilities that were up to standard. She tried to get more training in Chicago but was twice rejected by Rush Medical College. Finally, Chicago Medical College allowed her to take a year of classes, after which they granted her a degree since she was already a practicing physician. But she was the exception: after her single year there, the college once again refused to admit women.

In 1871, Dr. Thompson opened the Women's Hospital Medical College in Chicago at 141 North Clark Street. In a bitter reversal of fortune, it existed for only four days at this location before the fire of 1871 destroyed it. Undaunted, she later opened a new college, and in 1874 the first school of nursing was added.

There was a critical need for a hospital especially for women and children, so in 1865 Dr. Thompson opened one.

---

3 Walk farther west on Washington to La Salle.

At 166 West Washington, an earlier building housed the offices of the Women's Trade Union League (WTUL). Founded in 1903, this women's organization played a crucial role in encouraging women to join unions. It lobbied for legislation that would protect women from the exploitation that was rampant in the workplace. The League was also a key organization in the fight for women's suffrage.

This Chicago branch of a national organization was one of the most active in the country, with a unique mix of upper class and working women, academics, and reformers. Early members included Jane Addams, the founder of Hull House, and Mary McDowell, a co-founder of the WTUL and its president until 1907. Mary was also head resident of the University of Chicago Settlement.

1868–1945 MARGARET DREIER ROBINS

> One result of the 1910 men's clothing strike was the introduction of arbitration procedures, a giant step in the history of American labor and for Margaret a lasting achievement.

For many years **Margaret Dreier** was active in social reform in New York, but at the age of thirty-seven her life changed when she met Raymond Robins. This unusual man had worked in the lead mines in Colorado, made a small fortune in the gold rush in Alaska, and was an ordained minister in the Methodist and Congregational churches. As a lawyer, he had been the lead negotiator for the United Mine Workers union during a terrible and brutal strike in the anthracite mines in 1902.

When Margaret met him in 1905, Robins was the head of Northwestern University Settlement in Chicago. They agreed that marriage would not hinder either one of them; each would be free to work for social justice causes in the ways each thought best. Robins had good connections with the progressives at Hull House and throughout the city who wanted to see conditions change for the better among the poor, immigrants, workers, and women, and his contacts provided Margaret with immediate entry. She had become a member of the Women's Trade Union League in New York and quickly joined the Chicago branch. She soon became head of the Chicago WTUL and then of the national organization, which she served as president from 1907 to 1922.

Most unions in the United States at the time were organized according to trades and were hostile to women becoming union members. The League was organized to help working women become part of the trade-union movement. Its educational mission sought to inform the general public about the conditions of work and the difficulties that women faced in the workplace. There was a political mission as well: to work for permanent change through legislation that would protect women workers, especially regarding such issues as a minimum wage and maximum working hours.

One of the most famous strikes in Chicago labor history was at the men's clothing firm of Hart Schaffner and Marx during the winter of 1910–

1911. The garment workers faced incredible hardships during the long strike, and Margaret Robins helped to raise $70,000 to aid them. She secured legal counsel for the strikers and also marched on the picket line herself, and she worked hard to gain sympathy and support for the strike by making sure the public knew the workers' side of the story. One result of this strike was the introduction of arbitration machinery to solve grievances between workers and management, a giant step forward in the history of American labor. Margaret considered arbitration to be one of her major achievements.

Margaret Dreier Robins also worked diligently for women's suffrage, which she saw as a necessary extension of the American Revolution. She believed that the suffrage and labor movements should each understand that they were working for similar goals, and they should support one another. Despite her best efforts, however, the mostly middle-class suffrage movement failed to understand the needs of working-class women and trade-union organization.

1880-1948 AGNES NESTOR

Ill health had made schooling intermittent for **Agnes Nestor,** and it ended altogether in 1897 when she was seventeen, and an eighth grader. At that time, her father was out of work and had moved his family from Michigan to Chicago, so Agnes and her sister went to work to help support the family. Agnes worked ten hours a day at the Eisendrath Glove Company. There was no set or minimum wage; she was paid by the number of pieces she finished each day. In addition, she had to pay for the electric power her machine used and for any needles that broke.

The women at the factory often went on strike when their wages were cut, and Agnes, at eighteen, became a leader. Together with some of the male workers, they organized Glove Makers Local 1 in 1901, following a successful strike. But the women workers wanted their own group; they felt a separate union would represent them better, because women and men worked at different jobs. Moreover, in mixed unions, men took the leadership roles and dominated the decision-making. So the women proceeded to organize Local 2, and Agnes immediately became its president.

When the International Glove Workers Union was founded in 1902 at a convention, Agnes became one of only a few women to hold a national leadership role in a trade union. From 1903 to 1906 she served as third vice-president and a member of the executive board of the International. For the next seven years she had a paid position as secretary-treasurer and then, in 1913, she was elected president. That same year, she also became president of the Chicago branch of the Women's Trade Union League, the first working-class woman to hold that office. She retained the position until her death in 1948.

When the International Glove Workers Union was founded in 1902, Agnes became one of only a few women to hold a national leadership role in a trade union.

The union did improve the lot of the glove workers: they won better piece-rates; charges for power and needles were eliminated; and rates for overtime work were raised. Agnes thought this last was especially important. The long hours that women worked were injurious to their health, she felt, and she hoped that a higher overtime pay scale would reduce such hours. Her own health had been adversely affected by overwork, and physical breakdowns required her to take days off from time to time. In the end, the eight-hour-day law was not passed in Illinois until 1937.

Her Catholic, working-class roots helped to make Agnes a lifelong Democrat; by contrast, most women reformers tended to be from middle-class, Protestant, Republican backgrounds. When the Democrats held political power in Washington, Agnes Nestor was often called on to serve on advisory committees. During World War I, for instance, the government needed to encourage women to take on a variety of new jobs in factories and industry, and Agnes served as the only woman on a seven-member committee advising the Secretary of Labor. She used this position in 1920 to help create the Women's Bureau of the Department of Labor and to see that Mary Anderson, a long-time activist in the WTUL, became head of the Bureau.

1892-1964   IRENE McCOY GAINES

With a degree from Fisk Normal School in Nashville, Tennessee, **Irene McCoy** returned to Chicago in 1910 to look for work. Her Fisk degree qualified her as a teacher, and certainly she was over-qualified to be a clerk. Nevertheless, she was turned down everywhere she applied. The only employment offered to her was as a domestic. Irene took the job.

This experience reinforced what Irene already knew personally about discrimination against African-Americans, especially against African-American women. She would spend the rest of her life working fulltime, raising a family, and as an active volunteer in civil rights causes. She actively recruited African-American women to join the Women's Trade Union League. As a member of the Illinois Federation of Republican Colored Women's Clubs, she helped elect Ruth Hanna McCormick (see Tour I) to public office. Her volunteer work was in and through women's clubs.

The first women's clubs in the United States were organized in 1868, shortly after the Civil War. The early clubs concentrated on such subjects as literature, art, or gardening. The concept spread like wildfire, especially in cities, and soon there were clubs concerned with social problems and public affairs. The Women's City Club of Chicago, of which Irene was a member, was such a group. She was president of the National Association of Colored Women's Clubs, founded in 1898, for three different terms.

> As president of the Chicago Council of Negro Organizations for almost fifteen years, Irene led early battles for prison reform.

As president of the Chicago Council of Negro Organizations for almost fifteen years, Irene led early battles for civil rights. The organization fought for the right to serve on juries and for prison reform, and it sponsored literacy classes for domestic workers. In 1941, Irene led a delegation of fifty Chicago clubwomen to Washington, D.C. to protest racial discrimination in Federal Housing Authority programs as well as in New Deal work relief programs like the Civilian Conservation Corps (CCC) and the Works Progress Administration (WPA). The delegation also protested employment discrimination in industries that held government contracts and in various labor unions.

While there was no immediate response, after labor organizer A. Phillip Randolph threatened President Franklin Roosevelt four months later with a massive march on Washington, Executive Order 8802 was drawn up which forbade discrimination in companies that were doing business with the federal government. This was an important initiative: for the first time, large numbers of African-American women employed as domestics had an opportunity to get better paying jobs in factories.

Walk south on La Salle Street to the southwest corner of LaSalle and Monroe.

This was the location of the Women's Temple, built in 1893 by the Women's Christian Temperance Union, the WCTU. The building was twelve stories high and had seven elevators and three hundred offices. It was torn down in 1929.

1839-1898 FRANCES ELIZABETH CAROLINE WILLARD

Although **Frances Willard** trained to be a teacher, she became more and more convinced that serious reform was needed if women were to become equal to men, economically and politically. When the Women's Christian Temperance Movement was organized in 1874, Frances had just resigned from her position as dean of the women's division of Northwestern University—after disagreeing with the university over how the division was to be run—and she was asked to become the president of the Chicago WCTU. She worked for no pay at first, but she needed to support herself and her widowed mother. The problem was solved when Matilda Carse (see below), an active WCTU member, was able to raise and guarantee $100 per month.

> Under her leadership, the WCTU became much more than a single-issue organization.

The WCTU is often thought of as a single-issue organization, but under Frances Willard's leadership it became a force for liberal reform, advocating women's suffrage; the reform of the institutions of marriage, home and family life; and economic and religious rights for women. It also supported trade unions and protective labor legislation. A powerful speaker, Frances exhorted women to develop themselves and to participate in public life. After she became president of the national WCTU in 1879, it grew to more than two hundred thousand members by the turn of the century.

Cracks in the façade of the giant organization began to appear in the 1890s. Frances had become too liberal, gone too far ahead of her organization. Then the economic panic of 1893 ushered in a period of hard times. Frances became involved in reorganizing the British WCTU and began to spend six months of each year in England.

The national WCTU was one of the few reform organizations in America that welcomed African-American members, but when lynching was at its height and Frances was asked to take a public anti-lynching stance, she waffled. Worried about the opinions of the Southern white women in her organization, she recited the same justification that they gave: that lynching was necessary for the safety of white women. Since she had been a vocal advocate for Turkish refugees and humanitarian causes worldwide, her reputation suffered. It must be said, however, that very few reformers or social reform organizations during this so-called Progressive Era in American history were willing to take on the ugly and deep-rooted problems of racism.

Frances Willard died in 1898 as she was about to embark on another trip to England. More than two thousand people attended her funeral in New York, and many more came to pay their respects as the train carrying her body traveled through towns and villages en route to Chicago. She lay in state in the Women's Temple for a day, visited by an estimated twenty thousand additional mourners.

1835-1917 MATILDA BRADLEY CARSE

Widowed at thirty-four, **Matilda Carse** received an inheritance that was sufficient to take care of her three children and herself. After a drunken man driving a cart ran over her youngest son and killed him, Matilda began to work for temperance reform. It was she who raised the money to pay Frances Willard for her work as president of the Chicago WCTU, and in 1878 she succeeded Frances as president of the Chicago group. She served in that position for thirty-five years.

Matilda expanded the local organization's agenda. It operated two day nurseries for the benefit of children and their working mothers. It established a low-cost lodging house and a restaurant for young working girls. It opened an industrial school and a Sunday school, medical dispensaries, and a mission for "wayward" girls. Matilda also started a publishing arm of the WCTU, printing thousands of pamphlets. The publishing operation was a female-owned stock company which paid an annual dividend of seven percent and employed more than one hundred women.

All of this activity was in addition to the construction of the Women's Temple, a building that was paid for by women. WCTU members were asked to send one dollar each; Matilda herself raised $1 million. The impressive building was completed in 1893, the year that a severe depression swept the nation. The WCTU was unable to keep the building, and eventually it was torn down.

1860-1924 LUCY GASTON PAGE

With her father an abolitionist and her mother a member of the WCTU, **Lucy Page** possessed a reform agenda before she could spell the words. She became a lifelong crusader against the evils of cigarettes.

As a young woman, Lucy had begun teaching in a series of small Illinois villages, and in each place she saw boys running off to smoke behind the schoolhouse. She became convinced that there was a connection between their bad habit and their failure on exams. Moreover, she thought that once a boy started smoking, the next step would be drink. She also believed that cigarettes caused health problems.

At the time, the manufacture of cigarettes was a new industry in America. Only one percent of the tobacco consumed in the United States was in the form of cigarettes, but this new kind of smoking was mass-produced and mass-marketed. Access was easy; unlike a good cigar, cigarettes were very affordable. Lucy's crusade against cigarettes caught the attention of Frances Willard, who recommended her for a job in the WCTU's Department of Christian Citizenship.

Initially, the anti-cigarette campaign was fairly successful: between 1893 and 1921, fifteen states banned the sale of cigarettes. World War I was a major turning point, however. The federal government supplied cigarettes to soldiers despite the argument made by Lucy and others that if soldiers had to die, they should die "pure."

One important victory Lucy had was to get the

SIDE TRIP

At Madison Plaza, 200 West Monroe Street, there is a dark sculpture called Dawn Shadows. *This work in steel is by New York sculptor Louise Nevelson, who is often inspired by urban life. It can be viewed from any angle but is best seen from the elevated tracks above—an appropriate spot, since Nevelson described the sculpture as a response to the steel structures supporting the network of elevated tracks that surround Chicago's Loop.*

Chicago City Council to ban cigarettes containing ingredients like opium, belladonna, glycerin, or morphine. By 1924, the year that Lucy died after she was run over by a streetcar, only the state of Kansas prohibited cigarette sales.

 Walk east on Monroe to State. On the southeast corner you will see the Palmer House Hilton hotel.

1849-1918 BERTHA HONORE PALMER

The Palmer House is the oldest hotel in Chicago; the building you see is the third on this site. The first was ready for occupancy just days before the 1871 fire when, with the rest of the Loop, it was completely destroyed. Working feverishly, even using calcium lights so that builders could work at night, the second building arose. It was luxurious, with marble and mosaics. To some, it seemed overwrought. But it was home to **Bertha Palmer**, her husband Potter, and their two boys until they built an impressive home on north Lake Shore Drive in 1885.

Bertha quickly became the queen of Chicago society. She was an active participant in several of the city's most prestigious women's clubs—the Chicago Society for the Decorative Arts, the Fortnightly, and the Chicago Women's Club. After her castle-like mansion was built, she gave annual charity balls with hefty admission fees; they were the social events of the season.

With her connections, wealth, and prestige, it is little wonder that Bertha became the president of the Board of Lady Managers of Chicago's first world's fair, the Columbian Exposition of 1893. There was some opposition from a group who called themselves the Isabellas, after the Spanish Queen Isabella who financed Columbus's voyages to the New World. This group's membership of middle-class and professional women felt strongly that the celebration of women's accomplishments should not be separated from the exhibits of the achievements of men. But they didn't stand a chance.

The Board of Lady Managers moved quickly to commission a Woman's Building at the fair, to be designed by Sophia Hayden, a Boston architect and graduate of the Massachusetts Institute of Technology. Bertha Palmer lobbied effectively in Washington to get adequate funds for the women's committee. She used her own money to travel to Europe to convince royalty and women in high positions in many countries to sponsor or create exhibitions that would highlight the accomplishments and skills of women in those countries. She also commissioned art work and murals for the Woman's Building (see Tour III, Sara Hallowell).

More than eighty thousand articles were exhibited in the Woman's Building. In addition, work by women was included in other exhibits throughout the fair. Women were among the artists exhibiting in the Fine Arts Building, and their work was shown in the Department of Charities & Correction and the Department of Health buildings. Almost half of the exhibits in Horticulture were by women, as well as twenty-six percent of the exhibits in Fisheries and one hundred and twenty-five exhibits in the Department of Transportation.

Bertha and her board did not stop at the Woman's Building; they also raised money for a Children's Building which featured a model nursery that they constructed and operated. They set up a Woman's Dormitory Association to provide working-class women with affordable and safe accommodations during the fair. They organized a variety of lectures given at the Woman's Building throughout the six months of the exposition, and they sponsored the Congress of Representative Women (see Tour III). All of these activities combined to affect the lives of unknown numbers of women and were a major step forward on the long road to equality.

Bertha Palmer herself became an ardent art collector. Within a short time she owned ninety paintings by impressionist artists such as Claude Monet, Auguste Renoir, and Camille Pissarro, most of which she gave to the Art Institute of Chicago. There is no question that she was a good manager: after the death of her husband, Potter, in 1902, she was able to double his very considerable fortune in ten years.

Bertha had connections, wealth, and prestige; no wonder she became the president of the Board of Lady Managers of Chicago's first world's fair.

1893–1977 MERRIEL ABBOTT

SIDE TRIP

The Empire Room of the Palmer House is now closed, used only for special occasions, but the Beaux Art lobby of the hotel is worth a visit. Take an escalator to the second floor. (The stairs and entrance to the Empire Room are on the east side of the large, open lobby.) The hotel sometimes displays artifacts from its past in display windows along the ground-floor corridor.

She taught Ginger Rogers and June Taylor (the June Taylor Dancers performed at Radio City Music Hall in New York City), as well as hundreds of others at her dance studio in Chicago's Loop. Would-be dancers flocked to **Merriel Abbott's** school, and she had more than a hundred students from whom to choose for her renowned Abbott Dancers. The troupe not only was booked into those downtown Chicago movie palaces that offered a live stage show along with a first-run movie, but it also toured all over Europe and Latin America. The carefully supervised dancers had classes in grooming and etiquette, and Merriel also made sure that they continued their education while touring; she even enhanced it with French lessons.

The Abbott Dancers were a fixture at the Empire Room after it opened in the Palmer House hotel in 1933, and soon Merriel was booking all the entertainment for the room. After Conrad Hilton bought the hotel in 1945, he quickly made her director of entertainment for all of his hotels. She traveled the world looking for new talent and introduced Chicago audiences to entertainers like Edith Piaf, Tony Martin, and Jimmy Durante and dancers like Cyd Charisse and José Greco. In Hollywood, Merriel Abbott choreographed several Jack Benny movies using her Abbott Dancers, and she worked with Busby Berkeley. She developed dance routines for Judy Garland and Mickey Rooney, and she also supplied dancers for several Broadway musicals.

By 1955 there were no dancers available whom she herself had trained, and so she began to hire others. But she was disappointed with the training that these "outside" dancers had received, and she disbanded the Abbott Dancers in 1957. They had opened every show at the Empire Room for twenty-two years.

The following year, at the age of sixty-five, Merriel retired from her position with the Hilton hotels.

Hilton re-hired her as an independent agent, and she continued to book shows for him, such as the Ice Capades at the Boulevard Room in the Hilton hotel on South Michigan Avenue. Merriel kept her office in the Palmer House and worked at Hilton hotels worldwide until her final illness in 1977.

The New Kids on the Block

Across the street from the Palmer House, the northwest corner of State and Monroe was the site of a well-known department store, The Boston Store.

Today, giant "big box" discount stores threaten small retailers and even traditional department stores. But in the 1880s and 1890s, department stores were the new kids on the block, considered unfair competition to dry goods stores, small "general stores," and hardware stores. Marshall Field's (now Macy's) was established in 1881 and opened its current building to great fanfare in 1902. State Street became the prime location for other department stores, including The Boston Store.

Employees in earlier retail establishments were required to do many tasks, such as lifting, stocking, and cleaning, and many of these functions required physical strength. In the new stores, there was a growing division between labor and clerical jobs, and sales positions required more interpersonal skills and little strength. They were thus suitable jobs for women, and this opened up a new avenue of employment that many women eagerly sought—even though department store wages were very low. Testifying against a bill on the minimum wage, owners admitted that they could afford to pay women a living wage and still make money—but to pay more was not necessary.

Cross to the west side of State Street at Monroe.

1867-1954 ## MOLLY ALPINER NETCHER NEWBURY

One of those who started as a clerk in a smaller store was **Molly Alpiner**, and that store became The Boston Store, owned by Charles Netcher. Molly loved the business and rose through the ranks to become the chief underwear buyer. She caught Netcher's attention, was courted by him, and married him in 1891, after which she was a stay-at-home wife and mother until Charles died suddenly, in 1904.

During her years at home, Molly had remained passionately interested in the business, and she now took over the management of the six-story store, the only woman to head a major department store at the time. She remodeled the store in 1907 and again in 1912 and 1915, giving her a sixteen-story building with four thousand employees.

One hallmark of the early department stores was service to the customer. Catering to lower-middle-class customers, The Boston Store was called "America's Greatest Family Store." Cigars were rolled and candy was made on the premises, along with pies, cakes, bread, and rolls. For children, there was a playroom that was staffed, allowing parents to shop alone in the toy department or visit the post office and postal savings bank. Or perhaps Father could visit the barbershop.

Salesclerks at The Boston Store received very small salaries, but they earned large commissions and had unique fringe benefits. Employee lunchrooms were not uncommon then, but Boston Store employees could also play tennis on full-size courts on the roof. In 1916, the press reported that Molly was providing a summer resort in Wisconsin where employees could vacation in rented cottages.

Solomon Neuberger was a paint salesman when Molly married him in 1913. (Later he changed his name to Saul Newbury.) He had an office in the store, although he was not involved with its management. As time passed, Molly's policy of cash-only payment was kept in place too long, one of the reasons—the Great Depression of the 1930s was another—for a decline in sales, and she sold The Boston Store in 1941. New owners made improvements, but it was too late to turn things around. The store closed two years later.

Walk north on State to the building at 40 South State, an important site for the following woman.

1863-1929 IDA PLATT

In 1894, **Ida Platt** accomplished a first: she became the first African-American woman to earn an Illinois license to practice law. Her achievement made national news.

By 1906, Ida had her own law practice, and she set up an office in a building at 40 South State Street. This very prestigious building contained many law and business offices, all of them owned by white men.

Ida successfully practiced law for thirty years at this location.

Walk north on State to Madison Street. The McVickers Theater, Chicago's second theater, was located at 25 West Madison. Housed in its basement was the Chicago branch of the United States Sanitary Commission (later known as the Northwestern branch).

1820-1905 MARY ASHTON RICE LIVERMORE

Together with her husband Daniel, a Universalist minister, **Mary Livermore** was an abolitionist. They were planning to move with other abolitionists to Kansas when their youngest daughter suddenly became very ill, forcing them to abandon their plans and settle in Chicago. Daniel purchased ownership of a religious newspaper and published it for the next twelve years.

Mary had written numerous articles for religious and women's publications in the East, and her name now appeared immediately under Daniel's on the masthead of the paper. While she continued to help him put out the weekly paper and to write articles for it, this work did not consume all of her energy. In the 1850s she spent six years working with Jane Hoge and other Protestant women to found the Chicago Home for the Friendless, the Home for Aged Women, and the Hospital for Women and Children to help solve some of the problems they saw.

Both Mary and Jane Hoge (see below) are best known, however, for their talent for raising money and their organizational skills in the chief volunteer relief organization in the north during the Civil War, the United States Sanitary Commission. They made tours of army hospitals and reported on conditions, and they organized a reliable system of distributing needed supplies. Writing more than a thousand letters a week, they made contact with—and in some cases organized—some three thousand local aid societies in the Midwest, all of which contributed to the regional group, which was known as the Northwestern Sanitary Commission.

Mary and Jane wrote more than a thousand letters a week and organized events to raise money to support Civil War relief work.

Jane and Mary inspired women to join together to work for a national emergency, and then they found ways to coordinate this massive operation. Of course, all of this required money, and so they invented a new method of raising funds, the Sanitary Commission fairs. Their first event brought in more than $80,000, the second more than $200,000. These events involved women from all of the states that had been carved out of the Northwest Territory.

After the war, Mary Livermore became a prominent spokeswoman for women's suffrage, organizing the first suffrage convention in Chicago in February 1869. She brought the national leaders of the suffrage movement, Elizabeth Cady Stanton, Susan B. Anthony, and Lucy B. Stone, to speak. That well-attended meeting resulted in the establishment of the Illinois Woman's Suffrage Association.

1811–1890 JANE CURRIE BLAIKIE HOGE

Jane Hoge moved to Chicago in 1848 when her husband became a partner in an ironworks business. She had given birth to thirteen children in the first seventeen years of her marriage, eight of whom survived to adulthood.

She arrived at a boom period in Chicago. Witnessing the population triple from thirty thousand to more than one hundred thousand by 1860, Jane saw the social problems multiply. She helped to establish the Chicago Home for the Friendless, which opened in 1858 and admitted destitute women and children without regard to race, creed, or nationality.

It was here that she met Mary Livermore, and they both served as board members. In addition to raising money and making policy decisions, members of the Home's board also went out into the streets to look for unfortunate women and children to bring to the Home. Jane often performed this task, and she remained committed to the Home for the next thirty-two years of her life.

During the Civil War, Jane brought considerable management skill and fundraising ability to her work for the Northwestern Sanitary Commission, along with a deep personal interest— two of her sons were serving in the Union Army. She traveled extensively, organizing new chapters, keeping up morale, and making speeches that told of conditions and needs that she witnessed firsthand when she and Mary Livermore toured the battlegrounds and field hospitals.

Jane Hoge was one of those who proved that women were needed to help care for the wounded and to assist in solving social and community problems. Through fundraising fairs and events directed to women, she showed that women could bring considerable financial resources and contribute their skills to improve conditions.

 Look across State Street to the southeast corner of State and Madison, where the architect Louis Sullivan designed a people's palace, the Carson Pirie Scott & Co. store. Notice the restored cornice and beautifully wrought design in metal that distinguishes the main entrance. The building entered a new period in 2007, following Carson's decision to close the flagship store.

1908-1984 EDITH RAMBAR GRIMM

Carson's was opened in 1903, and sixty years later **Edith Grimm** became a vice-president. She was the first woman to achieve that distinction in Chicago retail.

Edith had one good idea after another. She effected changes in every department in the store, starting with the telephone sales and mail ordering department. Her innovations of personal service and quick deliveries increased the revenues brought in by that department by more than $1 million.

Carson's bridal shop had an average of twelve customers each year until Edith personalized the service, making it a shop where wedding gifts could also be purchased and the bride could find any accessories she needed. Edith sent her trained assistants to the wedding itself, where last-minute alterations or other problems could be solved on the spot. By 1960, five thousand brides were clamoring for Carson's merchandise and services.

Edith Grimm also created the first college shop in the area, and she coined the term "casual clothes." She maintained that her business resembled show business: it needed a significant amount of drama, like that provided by selling swimsuits in Chicago's cold, snowy January and billing it as a "resort wear" show. Imported fashion shows were another innovation of hers; she hung travel posters all over the store and in the windows. In 1955 she even brought a London taxicab to Chicago.

1889-1968 RUTH HETZEL HARSHAW

A gifted teacher, **Ruth Hetzel** left Wisconsin to teach in the Chicago suburb of Winnetka. After she married Myron Harshaw, the couple raised their four children there. Then, early in the Great Depression, Myron lost his job in advertising, and when Carson Pirie Scott offered Ruth the job of creating an educational services bureau, she seized the opportunity.

Developing a love of books in children had been a passion for Ruth since her first days of teaching. The Hobby Horse Book Foundation was an innovative mail-order program that sent a book chosen by Ruth to each enrolled child once a month. She also developed fifteen-minute radio dramatizations of stories from children's literature. In conjunction with "The Hobby Horse

In an innovative mail-order program, Ruth chose a book each month to send to each child enrolled in the Hobby Horse Book Foundation.

Presents" program, she wrote a newsletter, thirty-five thousand copies of which were distributed monthly through the Chicago Public Schools. By 1946, twenty thousand children responded to an annual poll asking them to vote for a favorite book, and the following year the number doubled. On WBEZ, the Chicago Board of Education radio station, another of Ruth's programs, "The Battle of the Books," aired every Friday afternoon. Schoolchildren sent in questions about books, and contestants tried to identify titles and authors.

Local radio station WMAQ, an NBC affiliate, began to air Ruth's show in 1949 as a public service and under a new name, "Carnival of Books." Seventeen months later, NBC syndicated the program and broadcast it nationally, aiming to get children enthusiastic about the new book presented each week. The format had Ruth introducing the book, followed by a six-minute reading by a trained actor. Often there was an interview with the author, who had been sent to Chicago by the publisher. When Ruth taped her conversations with European authors in 1956, for example, among her guests were Astrid Lindgren, the author of *Pippi Longstockings*, and Laurent de Brunhoff, creator of the Babar books.

 From the main entrance of the former Carson's building, walk east on Madison to Wabash Avenue.

1868-1951   CAROLINE HEDGER

In the early part of her career as a doctor, **Caroline Hedger** worked to provide for the health needs of immigrant workers in Chicago's Stockyards neighborhood. She wrote articles describing the effects of overcrowding, poor ventilation, and pollution. She tried to alert the public to the medical consequences of long hours and insufficient wages, as well as the unsanitary conditions in the factories. She wanted to see the state of Illinois set standards for the health care of its citizens.

When she established her private practice in 1912, Caroline's office was in the Heyworth Building, at the southeast corner of Madison and Wabash. She advocated a holistic approach to healthcare, and she had an early understanding of the relationship between social problems and the people's health. In her writing Dr. Hedger accused the government of killing citizens by neglecting to legislate legal safeguards for their health.

> Caroline wanted the public to know about the terrible working conditions that immigrants suffered.

 Walk another block east on Madison and turn right onto Michigan Avenue. On the building at 8 South Michigan there is an historical plaque dedicated to the early work of the Sisters of Mercy.

1822-1854 MOTHER MARY AGATHA O'BRIEN

She was born in Ireland and joined the Sisters of Mercy as a lay nun. At that time, families that could afford it provided dowries for girls entering the convent—land, goods, or money—to contribute to the costs of running the convent and doing charitable work. Those with dowries were educated and became teachers, administrators, or nurses, while lay members of the order like **Margaret O'Brien** did the basic housework, laundry, and gardening.

When the Sisters of Mercy were asked to supply nuns to work in Pittsburgh, Pennsylvania, Margaret was one of those sent; she was twenty-one. En route, the American bishop who had asked for the nuns was so impressed with her intelligence and skills that he made sure that she became a choir sister rather than a lay nun. He later said that, given a chance, Mother Mary Agatha could rule a nation.

In 1846, five of the Pittsburgh nuns under the leadership of the twenty-four-year-old Mother Agatha made the further journey to Chicago, to serve the needs of its twenty thousand residents. For more than a year they all lived in a rude hut, fit only for two or three persons, while they tended the sick and built a school for

Sisters and soldiers in the Civil War

In 1846, five of the Pittsburgh nuns, led by twenty-four-year-old Mother Agatha, journeyed to Chicago to serve its twenty thousand residents. girls, one for boys, and St. Francis Xavier Female Academy, a post-grammar school. Tuition from the Academy supported the nuns and most of their work; of course, additional fundraising was needed. Local farmers donated food that the nuns distributed to the poor and to prisoners in the city jail.

Their success and growing numbers allowed the Sisters to establish a night school for adults who could not read or write. A little later they opened an employment bureau, as well as a place where young women who were working could have room and board. By 1851 there were forty-four nuns in the Chicago convent, and the Mercy Sisters were able to start an orphanage, three Sunday schools, and an infirmary that was the beginning of what became Mercy Hospital.

Eight years after she came to help the fledgling Chicago community, Mother Agatha died in an 1854 cholera epidemic. The Mercy Sisters dropped all their other work to nurse the stricken in the epidemic. In addition to Mother Agatha, the convent lost three other nuns, and the city of Chicago lost 1,424 citizens.

1816–1888 MOTHER MARY FRANCIS DE SALES MONHOLLAND

Mary Monholland was also born in Ireland, but her widowed father moved to New York City and started a wholesale grocery business that prospered. Mary took care of the household and her three younger brothers. After finishing elementary school, she attended a private academy to study arithmetic, bookkeeping, grammar, and Christian doctrine and then went to work for her father, keeping the company's books and ledgers.

Mary volunteered in an orphan asylum in New York City that was run by the Sisters of Mercy, and she decided that she wanted to join the order. Her father objected, because he depended upon her not only in his business but also for the care of her brothers, even though he had remarried. Mary obeyed his wishes until she was thirty-one and her brothers were self-sufficient. Then, in 1847, she joined the Sisters of Mercy in Chicago.

Even while in training, and before her final vows, Mary's age and skills had already marked her for a leadership role in the order. At a time when women could not own property in the state of Illinois, it was Mother Mary Francis who created a corporation so that the Sisters of Mercy could buy the land they needed for St. Francis Xavier Academy. She bought other property as well, including that on which the new Mercy Hospital was built.

Her duties were administrative, but Mother Mary Francis also insisted on engaging in hard labor. She brought in the kindling wood for Xavier Academy and cleaned out the fireplaces in the classrooms. She succeeded Mother Agatha as superior of the Chicago convent and was reelected twice, serving until 1867.

As the northern and southern states fought between 1861 and 1865 in the grueling and bloody Civil War, a dire shortage of nurses developed. At the beginning of the war, the only nurses available

> Women could not then own property in Illinois, but Mother Mary Francis created a corporation so that the Sisters of Mercy could buy the land they needed for Xavier Academy.

were those trained in Catholic or Protestant religious orders. Of the twelve Catholic orders that responded to the call for help, the Sisters of Mercy were the best prepared, chiefly because their training program had been set up by nuns trained by Florence Nightingale during the Crimean War. To support the nurses, Mother Mary Francis organized laywomen to assist the nuns at such places as Jefferson City, Missouri, and the battlefield at Shiloh in Tennessee.

Many Confederate war prisoners were sent to Chicago's Camp Douglas, located on property owned by Senator Stephen A. Douglas at 35th Street and the lake on the city's south side. It was the largest camp in the north, with more than twenty-six thousand men imprisoned there, and more than four thousand died. Needless to say, conditions were deplorable. Finally, in 1864 a civic committee asked Mother Mary Francis to investigate charges of inadequate food and neglect. She brought sisters in to nurse the soldiers, but they ran out of supplies. The War Department refused her requests, so she wrote to President Lincoln and got the provisions she needed—by presidential order charged to the War Department.

After her tenure in Chicago, Mother Mary Francis built several schools in Iowa and supervised additions to two hospitals for the mentally ill.

Walking south on Michigan Avenue, cross Monroe to take a look at the understated elegance of the upper floors of the building at 122 South Michigan.

Louis Sullivan designed this building, now home to National Louis University.

It may sound familiar to modern ears, but in fact the importance of pre-schooling and the idea that young children should be provided with an environment that would stimulate learning and physical development began very early. These ideas were the basic tenets of the kindergarten movement that became popular in the United States after the Civil War. In Chicago, that movement developed into what is now National Louis University.

1849-1927 ELIZABETH HARRISON AND
1836-1917 RUMAH AVILLA HULL CROUSE

On a visit to Chicago, **Elizabeth Harrison** learned about the movement for early childhood education and enrolled in a thirty-six week course at Alice Putnam's pioneering kindergarten training school. She taught, received more training, and sought to understand more about the theories of Friedrich Fröbel. He emphasized teaching pedagogy to mothers and advocated a comprehensive program for the physical, mental, and moral development of the child.

As a teacher at Alice Putnam's elite Loring School, Elizabeth hoped to put some of these ideas into practice, and she invited twenty-one mothers to a class. Only two mothers showed up, but fortunately one of them was **Rumah Crouse**. She was a wealthy woman who had spent long hours doing volunteer work for her church and had been one of the founders of the Baptist Missionary Training School in Chicago. Rumah believed in the importance of education and was impressed with Elizabeth's emphasis on the role that mothers should play in the education of their children.

Within a week, Rumah organized another speaking engagement for Elizabeth. The audience overflowed into a second room and was so excited about Elizabeth's proposals that Rumah promptly announced that a class would begin the following week. Tuition for the course was $2.50, a portion of which would benefit the Baptist Ladies Aid Society. Elizabeth was delighted when forty-five women enrolled.

> With the help of Rumah's organizational skills, Elizabeth opened the Chicago Kindergarten Training School in 1888.

With the help of Rumah's organizational skills, Elizabeth opened the Chicago Kindergarten Training School a year later, in 1888. She designed the curriculum and Rumah took over the administrative work of what would become the National Kindergarten and Elementary College, later known as the National College of Education and now National Louis University. Both women worked tirelessly to promote new pedagogical ideas and insure excellent training of both "kindergarteners" and their mothers. In 1894 they organized a Mother's Congress in Chicago, and twelve hundred people from all over the country attended it. After that, conventions were held every year. By 1897 the sponsoring group was known as the National Congress of Mothers—now the Parent Teachers Association.

1883-1956 EDNA DEAN BAKER

> Edna saw that mothers recruited by the government for war work needed nursery schools for their young children.

When Elizabeth Harrison retired in 1920, she handpicked **Edna Baker** as her successor. She was an excellent choice. At the time, the National College of Education (now National Louis University) was housed in five crumbling old mansions and carriage houses in a neighborhood that had declined and was in the epicenter of the 1919 race riots. Edna raised $1 million and took the radical step of moving the school north to Evanston. Two new buildings were ready to receive students in 1926.

Then the new school, its mortgages, and its resilient president found themselves in the midst of the Great Depression. Most school districts met the first shortfalls in their operating budgets by cutting kindergarten classes, and fewer classes created a surplus of teachers. College for young women was a low priority in most depression-era families, and National College's enrollment fell drastically. The school's president and board of trustees did everything they could to economize, and they were able to survive—in large part because of the commitment and dedication of the remaining faculty and staff.

World War II brought new challenges. There were shortages of every imaginable material, even paintbrushes. Enrollments declined by sixty percent in other teachers' colleges in Illinois and across the country, but National was able to keep eighty percent of its students. Edna saw the emergent need for nursery school classes for the children of mothers who were being recruited by the government for war work, and she quickly hired unemployed teachers to staff these new facilities.

Edna Baker was the president of National College for thirty years, retiring in 1949. During her busy and demanding career, she also served on national committees on early childhood education, wrote pamphlets, and gave many speeches.

This is the end of Tour II.

Tour Three

start: Michigan and Madison
end: Columbus and Congress
time: 1 hour with reading stops

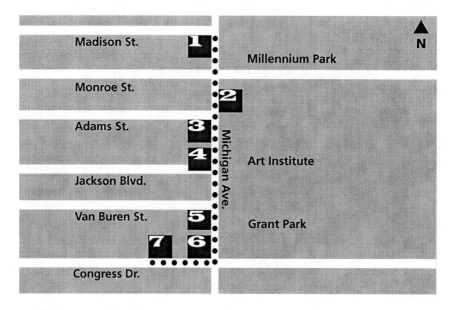

 Begin this tour at the corner of Michigan Avenue and Madison Street, and look east across Michigan.

As mentioned in Tour II, all the debris from the Great Fire was shoveled into the lake along this shore, a great start for a new "east side." Today, all of the area east of the Michigan Avenue roadway is made up of landfill.

"I Will" was the rallying cry of Chicagoans after the devastating fire of 1871. Rebuilding began immediately, and by 1872 they were so proud of their accomplishments that an interstate exposition was proposed. A huge building of iron and glass arose on what is now the site of the Art Institute of Chicago; it opened in 1873 for an eighteen-day industrial and agricultural fair. Afterward, since the building was available, the city held annual fairs there until 1890. In the following year, this "temporary" building was torn down to make way for the Art Institute.

Fifteenth annual opening of the Chicago Exposition Building, July 1887

1846-1924 SARA TYSON HALLOWELL

The first Interstate Industrial Exposition included works of art, and **Sara Tyson Hallowell** was listed as an art agent. In fact, it was she who introduced Chicagoans to the French impressionists. For ten years, Sara organized and managed art shows of four- to six-hundred paintings and related pieces. The last show, in 1890, included the work of Edgar Degas, Claude Monet, Auguste Renoir, and Alfred Sisley, among others. For the thousands of people who came to these art exhibitions, Sara also provided a first view of the work of Mary Cassatt and other important American artists such as William Merritt Chase, Childe Hassam, and Thomas Eakins.

In order to achieve the variety and quality that these exhibits displayed, Sara traveled extensively, coming to know artists and dealers in New York and Paris. She introduced Americans abroad to new art and artists, and she advised collectors like Bertha Palmer (see Tour II), whose extraordinary collection of impressionist paintings can now be viewed at the Art Institute.

When a man was appointed director of fine arts for the 1893 World's Columbian Exposition, Sara was deeply disappointed. Again she went to Europe, where she found Bertha Palmer traveling on behalf of the Woman's Building to be built at the fair. Sara introduced her to two expatriate American artists,

Mary Cassatt and Mary Fairchild MacMonnies, and Bertha lost no time in commissioning them to paint a huge mural apiece, for the ends of the great exhibition hall in the Woman's Building. Unfortunately, neither painting survives.

It was Sarah who introduced Chicagoans to the French impressionists.

As a special contribution to the Columbian Exposition, Sara assembled 132 masterpieces by foreign artists—works owned by American collectors—and these were shown in the galleries of the Fine Arts Building at the fair. After the exposition closed, Sara returned to France, but later, when the Art Institute began an annual exhibit of contemporary American artists, she became involved. From 1895 until the start of World War I in 1914, she pulled together the works of American artists then working in Europe for the Art Institute shows.

During the war, Sara volunteered at a hospital established by nuns to alleviate the wartime demand for medical and nursing care. She died in France in 1924, her enormous contributions to American cultural life almost forgotten. Only recently has new research restored her reputation and celebrated her groundbreaking work of championing impressionist and American artists and advising museums and collectors.

The Congress of Representative Women

Fairs like Chicago's 1893 exposition are of ancient origin. When they began, they usually were held in conjunction with a religious festival and had a commercial component as well, and the buying and selling attracted people from near and far. The first half of the nineteenth century saw the beginnings of national fairs, and the World's Fair of 1851 in London gets the most votes as the first truly "world's" fair. It was held in a single, gigantic space, the Crystal Palace. Other fairs that followed in major cities in Europe took place in similarly overwhelming exhibit halls.

Each showcased new building techniques and materials that could enclose vast spaces, and they demonstrated new manufacturing and industrial technologies. Only gradually did attention begin to be paid to nonmaterial aspects of civilization as well.

The Paris fair of 1889 included a series of intellectual and religious congresses that were a model for Chicago's Columbian Exposition. The Chicago planners—called the World's Congress Auxiliary—decided that international experts in many fields should address great themes. A woman's branch was also involved in the planning, of which Bertha Palmer was president and Ellen Henrotin vice-president. Ellen and members of her committee, which included Frances Willard, Myra Bradwell, and Sarah Hackett Stevenson, the latter a doctor and active advocate for poor women and children, did all the work, because Bertha Palmer was too busy with the Woman's Building. (See Tour II.)

The first meeting scheduled at the fair was the Congress of Representative Women, which took place May 15–21, 1893, in a vast new building, not quite finished, called the Art Palace—a building that later became the Art Institute. The main floor was divided into two large rooms, the Hall of Columbus and the Hall of Washington, while the rest of the building contained rooms of various sizes where smaller meetings could be held. Although the estimated capacity was twelve thousand persons, applications for meeting times and space were so numerous that it was extremely difficult to fit in all the topics that women wanted to hear about and discuss.

Opening day of the Congress strained the capacity of Columbus Hall; its entrances and hallways were choked with the middle-aged and elderly women who were characteristic of the audience. The rest of the week, double programs were prepared using both great halls. The agenda called for eighty-one sessions in all, and on occasion there were as many as eighteen meetings going on simultaneously. Total attendance at the Congress was estimated at 150,000, and many were turned away.

A Chicago woman reporter, sent to cover a speech on May 19 by the suffragist Susan B. Anthony, ran away from the disorderly throng on the steps. Instead of reporting on Anthony's speech, she wrote about the lace and jet beads and roses that were torn off her own dress and described how many umbrellas poked her in the ribs.

African-American women were excluded from an active role in planning the Congress of Representative Women, as well as from representation on the Board of Lady Managers. Nevertheless, they did participate in the Congress itself. Chicago's persistent Fannie Barrier Williams may have been the one to open the doors.

1855-1944 FANNIE BARRIER WILLIAMS

After debating for more than a year, the Women's Club finally let Fannie become a member.

A compelling and memorable speaker, **Fannie Barrier Williams** so impressed Ellen Henrotin at the Congress of Representative Women that Ellen nominated her for membership in the all-white Chicago Women's Club (later Chicago Woman's Club). The hostile and heated debate that ensued lasted for fourteen months. Fannie was finally admitted, but she was the only African-American member of the prestigious club for the next thirty years.

Fannie was an accomplished woman, a pianist, a writer, and an activist. She wrote for several newspapers and magazines and was a diligent worker in the women's suffrage movement as well as in the NAACP. Her participation was crucial to the founding of Provident Hospital and Training School in 1891 and in establishing the Frederick Douglass Center to promote better understanding and relations between races. In 1924, she was the first—and only—African-American appointed to the board of the public library.

Walk south on Michigan to Adams Street and look at the much expanded and landscaped Art Institute of today.

Two formidable lions guard the entrance, commissioned by Florence Lathrop Field and installed in 1894. The sculptor was Edward Kemeys, the first American to specialize in animal sculptures; he had executed several such sculptures for the Columbian Exposition. His wife, Laura Swing Kemeys, was also an accomplished sculptor. A large reception given for the Kemeys on May 10, 1894, celebrated the completion of the installation of the lions.

Students sketching plaster-cast reproductions, Art Institute of Chicago

The School of the Art Institute

When the Art Institute of Chicago (AIC) took over the exhibition building following the many congresses scheduled during the Columbian Exposition, it was not as a museum but rather as a school and gallery. AIC did not yet have a permanent art collection, and so the halls and spaces were filled with plaster-cast reproductions of classical statuary for the use of students.

Some years earlier, in 1866, fifty-five local artists had banded together to found the Chicago Academy of Design, which gave classes and provided gallery space for exhibitions. Students paid $10 per month in tuition fees, and instructors were paid $1,000 per year. Three years later, the Academy was on a firm financial footing, applied for a charter from the state of Illinois, and began to put up a building at 66 West Adams Street. The new building opened in November 1870, but the Great Fire swept it away in October 1871. After that, it was difficult for the Academy to get back on its feet. It rented rooms but did not have enough money to pay instructors, and its debt increased to $10,000.

The solution seemed to be to reorganize, so in 1879 the participating artists incorporated themselves under the name of the Chicago Academy of Fine Arts. The new organization prospered and in 1882 changed its name to the Art Institute of Chicago. Its first location was two blocks south, on the southwest corner of Michigan and Van Buren Street. When it outgrew that space, it commissioned the architectural firm of Burnham and Root to build a new structure of brown sandstone in the Romanesque manner at the same location, the site of what is now the Chicago Club.

In 1883 the school had 359 students; by 1893 this number had jumped to 929. Annual tuition had also increased, from $6,588 to $20,254. Again the Art Institute found that it needed more space, and it got permission to build on the lakefront. Fortunately, the organizers of the congresses at the Columbian Exposition were desperate for downtown space and agreed to assume some of the building cost of this final home.

1883-1974 LAURA VAN PAPPELENDAM

What is now known as the School of the Art Institute (SAIC) has had a distinguished roster of faculty. One was **Laura Van Pappelendam**, who came as a student and stayed to teach at SAIC for fifty years. She continued her education at the University of Chicago, where she helped to establish both the Department of Art and the Renaissance Club.

Laura also worked to encourage the university to include the study of art as a legitimate part of a liberal arts curriculum. She taught in the university's Department of Art after it was organized in 1924, while simultaneously maintaining her position at SAIC. Despite this heavy teaching load, Laura is best remembered as an artist. She won numerous awards and had her work included in 250 art exhibitions both here and abroad.

1878-1946 HELEN GARDNER

In the five years preceding World War I, **Helen Gardner** traveled to Greece, Egypt, and Europe, and those travels may have impelled her to return to the University of Chicago to get a master's degree in art history. In 1920 she became the first person to teach that subject at the School of the Art Institute, and a year later she was hard at work designing a complete art history curriculum.

Appropriate textbooks did not then exist, and so Helen wrote one: *Art through the Ages: An Introduction to Its History and Significance*. Her book helped students learn to really look at art, to identify basic design elements in a work, for instance, that might have originated in a different time period and/or a different culture. To sharpen students' awareness of the fundamental principles of design, Gardner and another SAIC teacher took students on field trips to the zoo, the aquarium, the Field Museum of Natural History, and the Oriental Institute on the campus of the University of Chicago.

In the next decade, Helen Gardner wrote a new book, *Understanding the Arts*, and she revised *Art through the Ages* to add sections on non-Western art, such as that from the Orient, Oceania, and Africa, as well as on prehistoric art from the Americas. This edition was not marketed solely as a textbook; an appreciative general public enjoyed it as well. Her work validated all art, not just that which was thought to be "classical" or part of a general canon.

An art historian, Helen taught her students how to really look at art—and wrote a definitive book to help.

1897-1988 KATHLEEN BLACKSHEAR

As a student at SAIC, **Kathleen Blackshear** took a class from Helen Gardner and found that the direction of her own thinking and work underwent a profound change. When she was hired to teach the survey course in art history, she followed Gardner's lead by introducing non-Western art and challenging students' assumptions and ideas about art. One result of this assault on perceptions was a Chicago "school" in the 1940s and 1950s that was composed of artists whose work was influenced by nontraditional sources. The group included such artists as Evelyn Statsinger, Leon Golub, and Seymour Rosofsky.

Unlike Gardner, an academic and writer, Kathleen Blackshear was also an artist of note. A series of paintings and other work depicting the lives of African-Americans are among her best-known works. An admiring art critic in 1954 called her one of Chicago's most talented and least appreciated artists.

1852-1887 ANNIE CORNELIA SHAW

A pioneering woman painter, **Annie Shaw** was one of the first women to obtain full status in the Chicago Academy of Design, the precursor to the School of the Art Institute. She was the first woman to open a studio in Chicago, which she did in 1874, and she exhibited her paintings at the Centennial Exposition in Philadelphia in 1876, the first opportunity for American women artists to showcase their work in a national setting.

Most of Annie's paintings were landscapes, and they sold for sums ranging from $5 to $800. At a posthumous exhibit of her work at the Art Institute of Chicago in 1889, a total of 270 paintings were listed in the catalog.

1867-1938 PAULINE LENNARDS PALMER

> She contributed her work to Art Institute shows for more than forty years.

The School of the Art Institute has had hundreds of students in more than a century of teaching and influencing the American art world. One, a prolific painter named **Pauline Palmer**, was as well known as Mary Cassatt was in her day. Pauline had studied on the east coast with William Merritt Chase, and her work was shown in the Fine Arts Building at the World's Columbian Exposition of 1893. Every year from 1896 to 1936, she exhibited in one or more shows at the Art Institute, except for 1934.

Pauline was the first woman to be given the honor of election as president of the Chicago Society of Artists; she served three terms, from 1918 to 1921. Her work was influenced by impressionism, and she painted landscapes and other scenes as well as sixty-eight portraits.

1909-1977 GERTRUDE ABERCROMBIE

A multitalented woman, **Gertrude Abercrombie** excelled in foreign languages, showed promise as a writer, and had an aptitude for music. As her college years came to an end, she found it hard to choose what she wanted to do. When she decided that she wanted to become a painter, she enrolled in the School of the Art Institute in 1929.

Her surreal work with its personal symbols is often linked to the 1960s imagists.

Portraits of Chicago Artists by Chicago Artists, an exhibit mounted by a gallery in 1932, gave Gertrude her first opportunity to participate in a professional show. The following year, she exhibited in the important Grant Park Art Fair and then, in 1935, at the Art Institute show, Artists of Chicago and Vicinity. She became successful and well known, living among artists, writers, and musicians. A jazz afficionada, she knew such jazz greats as Charlie Parker, Dizzy Gillespie, and Sonny Rollins.

Gertrude's work has been described as "surreal" or "magic" realism. Bit by bit, some of her obsessions and demons crept onto her canvases. A cat, an owl, some carnations, gloves, bunches of grapes, her personal symbols, were incorporated into her paintings. By the late 1950s it was apparent that she was mentally ill. Nevertheless, she left a bold and important art legacy. Her work is often linked with a Chicago group of painters called imagists who emerged in the late 1960s.

1913-1987 SARAJANE WELLS

In forty-five years of working life, **Sarajane Wells** had two very different and successful careers. While a student at Chicago's Senn High School, she took classes in acting and won the role of Betty, a cousin of "Jack Armstrong, the All-American Boy." She shared the hero's worldwide adventures in the radio show of that name, a daily program that first aired on Chicago's WBBM radio station in 1933. Sarajane played the role for thirteen years.

She studied at the School of the Art Institute for two years and then continued at Northwestern University. A tough director often sent her home in tears, and her father advised her to take direction or quit. This good advice resulted in the director giving her roles in several afternoon programs.

A charter member of the American Federation of Radio Actors (AFRA), Sarajane was part of a group called Bridge Was Up. The name echoed an excuse busy actors routinely used if they were late for a show, because they often had to rush from one radio station to another at a different location in order to play another role.

Daytime dramas, "soap operas," were born and bred in Chicago, and Sarajane had roles in "The Guiding Light," "The Woman in White," "The Road of Life," "The Right to Happiness," "The Romance of Helen Trent," and others. Occasionally she took all of the parts in a show, varying her voice, delivery, or interpretation so that listeners could distinguish characters. She had the lead in "The Woman in White" when the show moved to California in 1946, part of a trend that continued as shows moved to either coast and left the Chicago pioneers in the dust. After moving to California, Sarajane also acted in nightly dramas, winning a Peabody Award in 1949 for work in the "The Short Happy Life of Francis Macomber," a dramatization of an Ernest Hemingway short story.

As television became the new threat to radio, and opportunities for radio actors dwindled, Sarajane returned to Chicago. After clerking in a bookstore, she took a job as the head of the Education Department at the Chicago Historical Society (renamed Chicago History Museum in 2006). She brought a new vision and revolutionized programs at CHS and at other museums as well. Programming for children was her first priority, something that did not generally happen in the early 1950s. She introduced dramatic programs, hands-on exhibits, folk singing, storytelling, and costumed performers. Children could see multi-screen sound-and-slide shows.

Her richly varied talents enabled Sarajane to become both a popular radio actor and, ultimately, a dynamic museum educator.

More than thirty-one thousand children came to the CHS assembly programs. The Society's Education Department offered eighty-eight performances a year; in a two-year period it gave more than fifteen thousand tours and talks. Sarajane also developed volunteer and docent programs. She retired from the museum in 1959.

1890-1963 FRANCES M. FOY

When **Frances Foy** attended night school at SAIC, one of her instructors was the well-known artist George Bellows. She worked as an etcher, a printer, and a muralist, and her work was included in annual Art Institute exhibits for twelve years from 1929 through 1940.

During the Great Depression, Frances won an anonymous competition, the prize being a commission from the United States Treasury Department's Section of the Fine Arts, with four others to follow, funded by money from a set-aside program for improvements in public buildings. Frances and her husband, Gustaf Dalstrom, also an artist, worked on public buildings in Illinois, Wisconsin, and Indiana, including painting murals at the Chestnut Street Postal Station in Chicago.

Frances was not permitted to apply for work with the Federal Arts Project of the Works Progress Administration (WPA). The common assumption in the 1930s was that men were the breadwinners of families, and so federal relief organizations prohibited any woman from applying if her husband was part of the program. In effect this meant that Frances and many other women artists had reduced access to programs that were meant to help artists, even at a time when few private commissions were available.

Like most artists in America before World War II, Frances was a realistic painter. The same was certainly true for most public art during the depression. WPA murals and other public art of the period regularly depicted male figures; in the Midwest there were only twelve or so that had women as the main subjects or showed women without men. The work of Frances Foy was different; she often included more women than men in her paintings and usually depicted them as playing important roles. Prime examples are her murals in post offices in East Alton and Gibson City, Illinois; in Dunkirk, Indiana; and in West Allis, Wisconsin.

> In the 1930s it was assumed that men were the breadwinners, and federal relief organizations prohibited women from applying if their husbands were already enrolled.

1922-1983 MARGARET MARIE DAGENAIS

After studying at SAIC, **Margaret Dagenais** went on to teach at Loyola University in Chicago. She was also a working artist who focused on religious art and its relation to the liturgical reform movement in the Catholic Church in the mid-twentieth century. Margaret executed work for churches and chapels throughout Chicago. She did not want to produce art that would be appreciated by artists; rather, she wanted to make sure that ordinary people in a congregation would be stirred by seeing good art.

1871-1942 JULIA BRACKEN WENDT

The five women who worked on sculpture for the fair became known as the White Rabbits.

For many years, the famous sculptor Lorado Taft taught at SAIC, and most of his students were women. Taft demanded that his students learn to carve marble, a very unusual requirement at the time. When he received several commissions for sculpture for the Columbian Exposition, Taft realized that he would be unable to complete all the work and went to see Daniel Burnham, architect and chief planner for the site and buildings of the fair. He told Burnham that he would be unable to finish unless he put some young women from his classes on the job, as well as women sculptors who worked in his studio. Burnham said that he didn't care who did the work—Taft could use white rabbits if he wanted to—as long as it all got done. Thereafter, the five women sculptors who worked with Taft on projects for the fair were called the White Rabbits.

Julia Wendt was a White Rabbit. She had run away from home at the age of thirteen and become a domestic worker. At sixteen she received her first commission when she was asked to carve a church pulpit. It gave her the money that allowed her to enroll in SAIC, where she studied with Taft and soon became one of the assistants in his studio. He maintained a large studio and was very supportive of the women students, allowing them to work on his large-scale public projects.

In addition to working on the Taft commission to decorate the Horticultural Building at the exposition, Julia was asked to do *Faith*, one of six figures on the Illinois State Building at the fair. Each of the White Rabbits got independent commissions for these statues. They were each paid $800, and the commissions ignited their professional careers.

In 1909 Julia had a show of her work, together with the paintings of William Wendt, her husband. Both of them received many commissions as a result. Her marble bust of Dr. Sarah Hackett Stevenson (Tour II) used to be on display in the gallery of American art at the Art Institute.

Very few works of Chicago women artists and sculptors are available for public view. The book Women Building Chicago 1790–1990: A Biographical Dictionary *(Rima Lumin Schultz, Adele Hast, et al., eds., Indiana University Press, 2001) includes a special ten-page illustrated supplement in color of the work of most of the artists discussed here.*

1872-1955 BESSIE ONAHOTEMA POTTER VONNOH

Another White Rabbit, **Bessie Potter**, had been paralyzed from the age of two until she was ten. She underwent many painful treatments, but finally her doctor gave up, saying that there was nothing more that he could do. Ironically, she began to get better.

When she was fourteen, Bessie decided that she wanted to become a sculptor. An only child, she moved in 1877 to Chicago with her widowed mother. Bessie's mother worked as a clerk to support them, and Bessie enrolled in SAIC that year. Because her mother could only afford one year of tuition, Lorado Taft allowed Bessie to work on Saturdays as an assistant.

As mentioned above, the Art Institute was full of reproductions of classic statuary, and these remained part of the collection

> Bessie's "Potterines," small clay figures of Chicago women, were greatly popular during the Exposition.

until the 1950s, when the public objected to the idea of reproductions in an art museum. In any event, the first sculptors in the United States worked in the classical style, portraying their subjects as heroes and showing them in classical robes. Lorado Taft and Augustus Saint-Gaudens were the first Americans to challenge this tradition, showing their subjects in natural poses and wearing contemporary clothes. Bessie Potter was in full agreement with this approach.

The Columbian Exposition was very important to sculptors and artists in America. Bessie rode to the grounds every day in an unheated, horse-drawn car and thought herself very lucky. She was disappointed that she did not get work on the Woman's Building at the expo, but in addition to the work with Taft she sculpted an eight-foot figure portrayed with palette and brushes, entitled *Art*, for the Illinois State Building. She also executed two plaster busts for the Fine Arts Building.

Archeologists in Greece at the time had discovered some exquisite, small terra-cotta figurines. Perhaps influenced by the popularity of these statues, Bessie made one hundred twelve-inch figures of Chicago women. Adding color to the clay, she depicted the women in the clothes they wore when they sat for her. The great popularity of these statues, called "Potterines," was partly due to Bessie's connections with various Chicago women's clubs. One such group, the Arche Club, donated money to the Art Institute for the purchase of seven works by Potter. None are currently on view.

In 1899, Bessie married a painter, Robert Vonnoh. She was able to balance her household and professional duties because her mother lived with the couple; they did not have children. Over the next two decades, she won many awards. In 1913, President Woodrow Wilson's wife, Ellen, asked Bessie to exhibit some of her work in the White House. She was the first American artist to have a display there.

In the last years of her life, Bessie liked to sculpt figures of children and adolescents in a garden setting. One example of this work is in the Theodore Roosevelt Bird Sanctuary in Oyster Bay, New York.

1886-1974 MABEL LANDRUM TORREY

Beginning as a student of Taft's at SAIC, **Mabel Landrum Torrey** went on to work in his Midway Studio in the neighborhood of Woodlawn, on Chicago's south side. She worked there for fifty years, and she lived in the community as well. Much of her skillful work portrayed children, real or idealized, as charming and appealing.

Mabel's training was classical in method, and she continued to work in that way while rejecting the trends of mid-century sculpture which often celebrated mass and machine-like finishes. She preferred the subtlety of hand-worked clay. Her most available—and most famous—work is the *Wynken, Blynken, and Nod* fountain in Denver, Colorado.

1874-1973 NELLIE VERNE WALKER

Because her father was a maker of tombstones, **Nellie Verne Walker** learned to carve stone at an early age. Then, in 1893, she was among the millions who came to see the wonders of the Columbian Exposition. Nellie also saw sculpture, and she resolved to study at the School of the Art Institute. But she had no money, and so she returned to Iowa and became a secretary to a lawyer. It took her six years to save enough money to come back to Chicago, and even then she struggled to survive. She received a small salary as an assistant to Taft, and in 1904 she became an instructor in clay modeling at the school.

In 1905, the book *Art and Progress* featured a cemetery monument that Nellie carved, along with works by Daniel Chester French and Augustus Saint-Gaudens and others. She did fourteen more monuments with partial figures emerging from rough blocks of granite. Her best-known work is a statue of the Indian Chief Keokuk in Keokuk, Iowa. Her strong work was often compared to that of Auguste Rodin.

When Lorado Taft died in 1936, Nellie was one of the five associates named to complete the

> Her strong work was often compared to that of Auguste Rodin.

commissioned works in progress in his studio. The Heald Square monument on East Wacker Drive at Wabash Avenue, completed in 1941, is a memorial to George Washington, Robert Morris, and Hyam Salomon. Leonard Crunelle worked from Taft's small model for the overall design, and Nellie executed the figure of Salomon.

The Art Institute of Chicago

Since the main rooms of AIC were filled in the early days with groups of plaster-cast reproductions, there were very few paintings on exhibit; of them, perhaps only thirteen could be considered major works. One of these was *The Assumption* by El Greco. Mary Cassatt had found this painting in 1901, when she spent time in Spain early in her own painting career. She believed that it belonged in America and urged its purchase. It was thirteen feet high, and the painter was virtually unknown at the time.

When the painting was shipped to Chicago in 1906 for consideration, the AIC board made the bold decision to buy it; subsequently, the local press derided it. It was the first El Greco to be publicly displayed in the United States. The purchase price reportedly was $40,000, and several board members had to dig into their own pockets in order to acquire it. In 1917, Nancy Sprague made a donation that covered the cost and reimbursed the original lenders.

SIDE TRIP

A major work by Lorado Taft and his assistants is **The Fountain of the Great Lakes**, *a 1913 sculpture that adorns the south wing of the Art Institute on Michigan Avenue near Jackson Boulevard.*

Plaster-cast reproductions, Art Institute of Chicago

In 1922, four years after her death, Bertha Palmer's will provided for a significant contribution to the Art Institute, a major step toward turning it into an important and influential museum. Bertha had made her first purchase in 1889, buying a painting by Edgar Degas entitled *On the Stage* for $500. In the early 1890s she rapidly assembled an incredible collection of impressionist paintings. These were hung in the ballroom of her house on Lake Shore Drive, but her very favorite painting, *Two Little Circus Girls* by Renoir, hung in her bedroom, and she took it with her whenever she went traveling.

Many of Chicago's wealthy elite who were growing older began to follow Bertha's example by including AIC in their wills.

1858-1937 KATE STURGES BUCKINGHAM

Buckingham Fountain

Kate Buckingham spent much of her life taking care of her family. Her father was blind, her sister, Lucy Maud, an invalid, and her brother, Clarence, a bachelor. To amuse her sister, she once bought a Chinese snuff bottle when such objects first came on the American market, and soon she was collecting outstanding Chinese bronzes and porcelains.

Clarence first saw Japanese prints at that country's pavilion at the Columbian Exposition, and he came away with a new passion for these delicate works. He met regularly with four other collectors, and their combined collections, which totaled 649 prints, were shown in 1908 at the Art Institute. Frank Lloyd Wright designed the installation. It was said at the time that a show of such quality would have been impossible to mount anywhere else in the world, with the possible exception of Paris.

After Clarence died in 1913, Kate expanded his collection to more than fifteen hundred prints. Later, she donated her collection of Chinese art to the Art Institute in Lucy Maud's name and gave the Japanese prints in Clarence's name. Nothing was ever donated in her own name, including Buckingham Fountain (see p. 111). In addition, her will provided for a bequest of $2 million to the growing cultural institution that was AIC.

1856-1932 ANNIE SWAN COLBURN

From the time of her marriage until she died, **Annie Colburn** lived on South Michigan Avenue. Originally, the homes of wealthy and prosperous Chicagoans lined the street, but when the great fire destroyed these homes, many people moved away, out of the center of the city. The Drake family, however, built a luxurious hotel on the corner of Michigan and Harrison streets, and Annie moved there with her mother in 1910 after the death of her husband, a patent attorney. She remained there, a virtual recluse, until her death in 1932.

It was after her husband's death that Annie began collecting art. Her suite was drab and poorly lit, but the impressionist and post-impressionist paintings hanging on the walls and stacked around the rooms were drenched in color. Van Gogh's *Sunny Midi, Arles* was hidden under her bed because it was too bright.

Annie Colburn bought what she liked, as did most of the early Chicago collectors. She had no education or training in the arts; New York dealers would send paintings on approval, and she often kept them for six months or more. If she wanted more time, she would tell the dealer that she had not yet "seen" it. When she made up her mind, either the painting or a check would be in the mail.

In 1932, the Antiquarian Society of the AIC persuaded Annie to loan sixty-three paintings and watercolors for a special exhibit. None of the works had ever been outside of her apartment since she purchased them. Despite serious heart problems, she supervised the selection of each piece for the exhibit. Her collection included the work of Toulouse-Lautrec, Degas, Monet, van Gogh, Renoir, and Cezanne.

Annie was at the Art Institute for the opening reception. Afterwards, she went home without her paintings, and she never saw them again. Two months later she was dead. In addition to the paintings, Annie gave the AIC $150,000 for the care and maintenance of her stellar collection.

1870-1939 BESSIE BENNETT

From 1895 to 1898, **Bessie Bennett** was a student at SAIC and took classes in the design curriculum from Louis Millet, a partner in Chicago's most prestigious decorating and design firm. Bessie became a jewelry designer, but she also took a part-time job in SAIC's library and later worked as an exhibition clerk.

Before Bessie got the job of exhibition clerk, the person who ran the "museum" side of the Art Institute, William French, worked alone in a tiny office as curator, registrar, public relations person, and educator. Bessie became his assistant in 1906, and in 1914 she was made Curator of Decorative Arts, the first woman to become a curator at the Art Institute.

The Antiquarian Society, composed of wealthy, socially prominent women, was founded before

> In 1914 Bessie became Curator of Decorative Arts, the first woman curator at the Art Institute.

SIDE TRIP

Spend some time in the Art Institute. You can request a floor plan that will give the location of Decorative Arts, the Buckingham collections, impressionists and post-impressionists, and a recently expanded and redesigned American Art section.

the new AIC building was built, and its donations of antiques and decorative arts form the basis of the AIC collection. During the twenty-five years of Bessie's tenure, until 1939, the Antiquarians evolved into a support group for the American Arts and Decorative Arts departments. Bessie was able to convince Society members to purchase the items she believed belonged in the collection, as well as to donate money outright.

In the new building after the fair, exhibit space was enlarged, and Arts and Crafts exhibitions occurred annually. Bessie Bennett was a genius at display and exhibition, often using bold colors instead of the customary white background to highlight artifacts. The director who succeeded William French complained that Bessie was able to put a dishrag on display and make it look like it belonged in a museum. According to him, she frequently did.

Except for her three years at SAIC, Bessie had a very limited education. She represented the self-taught museum enthusiast, and she was anxious to educate the public. An eloquent speaker, she gave many talks throughout the Midwest. Bessie devoted her life to her job. In fact, she had a stroke and died immediately after a meeting with the president of the Antiquarian Society.

As the museum grew, subsequent directors wanted a professional staff with stronger academic qualifications. By the time Bessie Bennett died, the AIC had grown to five curatorial departments, had several hundred employees, and the departments of registration, public affairs, education, and publications all had separate offices.

 Walk south on the west side of Michigan Avenue to Orchestra Hall, at 220 South Michigan Avenue.

Until this building was completed in 1905, the Chicago Symphony Orchestra (CSO) gave its concerts in the Auditorium Theater (see below) for fourteen years. Finally, the orchestra's founder, Theodore Thomas, got his wish for a concert hall exclusively for the CSO. Thomas died in January 1905, just weeks before Orchestra Hall opened.

The new hall made it possible to give African-American composers of classical music some recognition, as was beginning to happen throughout the country in the first decade of the twentieth century. In Chicago, this took the form of special programs billed as All Colored Composers' Concerts that were given in the hall in 1914, 1915, and 1916. They featured African-American soloists, especially violinists and pianists, and compositions by African-American composers.

1883-1974 NORA DOUGLAS HOLT

Nora Holt was awarded the degree of Master of Arts in music in 1918 from Western University, perhaps the first African-American woman to earn such a degree. Even before that, she won the distinction of being one of only two women composers included in the All Colored Composers concert at Orchestra Hall in 1915. Her composition was a song entitled "Who Knows," music put to the words of a poem by Paul Laurence Dunbar.

Subsequently, Nora was a music critic, writing the first column of music criticism to be printed in an African-American paper, *The Chicago Defender*, which had a million readers. African-Americans had very little access to classical music at the time, and Nora hoped that her column would introduce readers to this kind of music and help to educate them about it. Although her writing was devoted primarily to classical works, she had a keen appreciation of jazz and blues. She believed that a love of music was a great equalizer between people and should be held in common among all races.

1888-1953 FLORENCE BEATRICE SMITH PRICE

The compositions of **Florence Price** first won public recognition in 1925 and 1926. Two pieces, "Memories of Dixieland" and "In the Land of Cotton," were quickly followed in 1928 by a public performance of her piano piece "At the Cotton Gin." Frederick Stock and the Chicago Symphony Orchestra included Price's Symphony in E Minor in a program in June of 1933, the first time that a composition by an African-American woman was played by a major orchestra.

That symphony, one of her best and best known, was also played at a special all-Price concert at Chicago's second world's fair, the 1933 Century of Progress. Stock conducted the CSO, and Price, an accomplished pianist, played several other works that she had composed. The following year, the Women's Symphony Orchestra of Chicago played her E Minor Symphony during the Grant Park summer concert series. Margaret Bonds, one of Florence's piano students, was guest soloist.

All in all, Florence composed an astonishing five hundred works. A few of her arrangements, sung by Marian Anderson and Leontyne Price, are available on recordings. Florence joined the American Society of Composers and Performers (ASCAP) so that some of her larger works would be available in manuscript form.

1921-1998 MARGARET HILLIS

At the age of five, **Margaret Hillis** began piano lessons; she started to compose music when she was seven-going-on-eight. By the age of nine, she knew that what she really wanted to be was a conductor.

A rigorous perfectionist, she built the CSO Chorus into a superb, Grammy-winning choral instrument.

Her first experience came when, having persuaded her high school music teacher that he needed an assistant, she volunteered to direct the sectional rehearsals. Soon she was holding rehearsals for the full band. On one occasion, she was allowed to prepare a piece of music and conduct it at one of the band's concerts.

An active teenager, Margaret rode horses, swam, loved to water ski, and was a junior golf champion. In 1941 she took flying lessons, because she wanted to join the Women's Auxiliary Service Pilots (WASPS), but she did not qualify because of poor eyesight. Disappointed, she became a civilian flight instructor for the Navy instead.

After the war, Margaret returned to Bloomington, Indiana, to finish college at the University of Indiana, where she studied musical composition with Bernhard Heiden. He encouraged her to go to Yale for graduate school and to study composition with Paul Hindemith, but Margaret responded that she wanted to be a conductor. There was no way that a woman could become a conductor, Heiden told her, but perhaps choral conducting might provide a way in through the "back door." So Margaret went to the Juilliard School in New York City and studied with Robert Shaw, eventually becoming the assistant conductor of his Collegiate Chorale.

In 1957 Fritz Reiner invited her to form the Chicago Symphony Orchestra Chorus. This was a unique challenge: even major orchestras could not afford to maintain their own professional choruses and generally used community or amateur groups— the Cleveland Symphony was the only exception at the time. After Margaret accepted Reiner's offer, she found that there was no professional choral activity in Chicago at all.

A rigorous perfectionist, she conducted the CSO Chorus for thirty-seven years, constantly having to struggle for singers, funding, and recognition. Her unflagging efforts built the chorus into a superb, flexible instrument that won nine Grammy awards, transformed the performance of choral music, and was a lasting influence on choruses throughout the United States.

In 1977, Margaret earned headlines in most newspapers in the United States. Sir Georg Solti was scheduled to lead the CSO in Gustav Mahler's massive and difficult Eighth Symphony in both Chicago and New York, but he fell and was unable to conduct. On the afternoon of the Saturday evening performance in Chicago, the request came to Margaret to conduct that very night. She declined because she had not worked with the soloists and did not know the work well enough, but she said that if needed she would conduct in New York on the following Monday night. And she did, directing more than four hundred singers and instrumentalists in this complex work and winning a standing ovation.

Although she had a few more opportunities to conduct before she retired in 1991, Margaret never fully realized her lifelong dream of heading a major symphony orchestra. In July 2005, the *Chicago Tribune* and other media announced that Marin Alsop had become the first American woman to do so, in Baltimore. Subsequent articles detailed some controversy surrounding her appointment. Alsop has created a foundation to give women opportunities to study conducting.

Making History Now

Jane Glover, *a renowned scholar and interpreter of early music, has conducted all of the major classical symphonies in England, her home, and elsewhere in Europe, Australia, and the United States. She became music director of Music of the Baroque in Chicago and a guest conductor for Chicago Opera Theater.*

Shulamit Ran *is an acclaimed composer who won a Pulitzer Prize in 1991 for her First Symphony; she is a professor of composition at the University of Chicago. From 1990 to 1997, she was composer-in-residence at CSO and, from 1994 to 1997, at the Lyric Opera of Chicago. Succeeding Ran as CSO's composer-in-residence was* **Augusta Reed Thomas,** *who held the position from 1997 to 2006.*

Next to Orchestra Hall is a gleaming white terra-cotta building, the Railway Exchange, later called the Santa Fe building.

1868-1965 CLARA BARAK WELLS

From 1936 to 1970 this building housed a crafts shop established by **Clara Wells**. A suffragist and a silversmith, she began her studies at the School of the Art Institute in the late 1890s. By the time she graduated in 1900, SAIC graduates were establishing crafts shops based on the ideas and principles of the British Arts and Crafts Movement. This social and artistic movement promoted a return to decorative arts that were handmade, unique, beautiful, and affordable.

Clara's shop was called Kalo, after the Greek word for beautiful. Together with a workshop, it was originally in the Fine Arts Building (see below) and remained there for more than three decades before Clara moved it to Michigan Avenue. She employed twenty-five silversmiths, and the shop became known for some of the most beautiful silver pieces ever made in America. New York's Museum of Modern Art asked her to send representative pieces for an exhibit that MOMA mounted in 1939.

Although Clara employed highly skilled craftswomen and designers, in fact she was the one who controlled the designs and what the shop would offer. After retiring in 1940, she continued as owner of the shop. In 1977, the Chicago Historical Society sponsored a comprehensive retrospective of the work of Clara and the other artisans who had been part of the Kalo shop.

Clara was also one of the founders of a club for women located in the Fine Arts Building. There was already a club there, the Cliff Dwellers Club, for artists, architects, and writers—but for men only. Lorado Taft was a member, as were Henry Fuller and Hamlin Garland. Because this elite group refused women membership, the women organized the Cordon Club in the same building. It wasn't until the 1990s that women were finally admitted to membership in the Cliff Dwellers Club, which by then was no longer in the Fine Arts Building.

> Clara's shop became known for some of the most beautiful silver ever made in America.

 Continue walking down Michigan Avenue.

On the southwest corner of Michigan and Van Buren, you will see a massive brown limestone building that housed the first Art Institute of Chicago. It is now the Chicago Club.

In the middle of the block, at 410 South Michigan, is the Fine Arts Building.

It was erected as a factory for the Studebaker brothers, who started out as carriage makers and later manufactured cars. The large windows showcased the carriages, and the arched doorways were large enough so that vehicles could be taken out of the showroom. When the Studebakers built a new factory elsewhere, the building was renamed the Fine Arts Building; it is an historical landmark and has sheltered many different groups. The Cordon Club met there, as did the first club in Chicago for women, the venerable Fortnightly. A number of suffragist organizations had offices in the building as well, and when women were marching down Michigan Avenue in suffragist parades, staffers and volunteers would hang out the windows to watch and cheer.

99

1859-1953 LOUISE DEKOVEN BOWEN

One of those parades occurred after the 1916 Republican presidential candidate endorsed equal rights. Five thousand Chicago women marched in praise of his courageous position, and **Louise Bowen** led that parade. She was the vice-president of the Illinois Equal Rights Association and the president of the Chicago Equal Rights Association.

Louise was a regal woman from a background of privilege. Her roots were sunk deep in Chicago history: she was a descendant of Fort Dearborn pioneers, and her maternal grandfather owned real estate in early downtown Chicago. She was a good friend of Jane Addams, who used Louise's contacts to good advantage in raising funds for Hull House. Louise herself was the largest contributor, giving the settlement house more than $500,000. She was especially interested in the welfare of children and lobbied for the establishment of the juvenile court. When the court opened, however, it quickly became apparent that no funds had been provided to pay probation officers. Louise paid them, and she also found homes for dependent and delinquent children.

Through this work, Louise became aware of the needs of the African-American community, the first reformer to do so. At her insistence, the Juvenile Protection Agency made an in-depth study of the effects of racism on education, employment, housing, law enforcement, and entertainment. The study set a pattern that became one of the hallmarks of the settlement movement and of the kind of social work that Jane Addams and her colleagues invented—aided and abetted by such progressive women as Louise Bowen: first, study the problem; do research; and then find solutions and take action.

1827-1884 KATE NEWELL DOGGETT

The founder of the Fortnightly Club in 1873 was **Kate Doggett**. It is one of the oldest women's clubs in America and the oldest in Chicago. Kate was the beneficiary of a rigorous classical education, then available only to a few young women in the country. Throughout her life she remained an intellectual and hungered for the life of the mind. She wanted to know everything that was worth knowing and to hear all that was worth hearing, and she founded the Fortnightly to give Chicago women that opportunity. Often there were guest speakers, but the members themselves were encouraged to write and present papers after doing rigorous research.

> She wanted to know everything that was worth knowing and hear all that was worth hearing, and she founded the Fortnightly to give Chicago women that opportunity.

Kate's other passion was equal rights for women. Her own experiences taught her that even a woman married to a man of means was limited in her rights and freedom. When her husband died in 1876, she found herself with few resources. The estate became entangled in liens and red tape, creditors had to be paid first, and she ended up with no access to any money, not even living expenses, until it was completely settled. She went off to live in Cuba, where she and her husband had enjoyed vacations and where she could live very frugally. Kate made a few visits to Chicago for meetings and to see friends, but she was unable to live her former life here. She died in Cuba in 1884.

A Chicago Renaissance

The Fine Arts Building was also the headquarters for a renaissance in Chicago that began shortly after the turn of the century and lasted into the early 1920s. It was a time when artists, actors, writers, and poets were trying to get rid of the conventions and limitations of the nineteenth century. They liked to quote Nietzsche and advocated cubism and free verse. The ideas of Sigmund Freud, psychoanalysis, and radical politics often got enthusiastic backing. Experimentation and risk-taking, the development of new forms, and lots of talk were the order of the day.

1886-1973 MARGARET ANDERSON

Although **Margaret Anderson** lived in Chicago for less than a decade, her work has had a lasting impact on Chicago's cultural life. Her magazine, the *Little Review*, brought the attention of a small but influential national audience to such Chicago writers as Sherwood Anderson, Floyd Dell, Eunice Tietjens, and Ben Hecht. She also published newly emerging poets and writers like T. S. Eliot, HD (Hilda Doolittle), and Amy Lowell.

Margaret was the first to publish, in serial form, James Joyce's new novel, *Ulysses*. Because the United States Post Office thought the book was obscene, copies of the *Little Review* were confiscated, and Margaret and Jane Heap were tried, found guilty of obscenity, and fined $100 each. The book, written in 1918, was not published in the United States until the 1930s.

A very attractive woman with a passion for literature and art, Margaret wanted the *Little Review* to be a platform for controversy and the newest ideas. Articles on feminism, tolerance of homosexuality, and anarchism appeared on its pages, as well as the ideas of Emma Goldman and other radical thinkers. The magazine's finances were always precarious, and it sometimes lost financial backing because of its fearlessness. Margaret titled the first volume of her autobiography *My Thirty Years' War*.

1883-1964 JANE HEAP

A good example of a Chicago Renaissance person was **Jane Heap**, who came to Chicago in 1901 and earned a degree in drawing and painting from the School of the Art Institute four years later. She left for Germany to study tapestry and mural design; on returning, she taught and also continued to take night courses at SAIC for two more years. Her paintings were shown in several local galleries and exhibitions and received favorable reviews. She painted murals in the homes of prominent midwestern citizens and also prepared murals for two public schools.

Jane was a member of several amateur theatrical groups, and in 1912 she joined Chicago's Little Theater as a set designer and an actor. After

Her witty and provocative columns in the Little Review *delighted and angered but never bored.*

meeting Margaret Anderson, founder of the *Little Review*, she was persuaded to become a writer. Her columns—witty, provocative, sharply critical—greatly influenced the *Little Review*. Some readers were delighted, others indignant, but few were ever bored.

The *Little Review* began publication in 1914 and ended in 1929. Jane was solely responsible for the publication during its last five years, and it became even more avant garde. She was more interested in the visual arts than Margaret had been, and the work of artists on the cutting edge, such as Frank Stella, Fernand Léger, Joan Miró, and Constantin Brancusi, appeared in its pages.

1882-1979 ELLEN VAN VOLKENBURG BROWNE

Two years after **Ellen Van Volkenburg** married Maurice Browne in 1910, they founded the experimental Little Theater in the Fine Arts Building. It was a repertory theater, with a mission to give Chicago audiences the most stimulating, shocking, and challenging theater possible. Clarence Darrow, Eugene Debs, Lincoln Steffens, Theodore Dreiser, and Emma Goldman all appeared on its stage. Poets like Harriet Monroe, Carl Sandburg, Vachel Lindsay, and Eunice Tietjens read their work.

> The experimental repertory theater in the Fine Arts Building gave Chicago audiences the most stimulating, shocking, and challenging theater possible.

Ellen and her husband brought European, English, and Irish plays to America; they were the first presenters of Ibsen's plays in this country. She wore many theatrical hats, as actor, producer, director, and writer. She also created the first serious children's theater in America and made the art of making marionettes more widely known.

The Little Theater had to declare bankruptcy in 1917, after which Ellen and her husband performed frequently on the West Coast and in London. In 1940, Ellen Van Volkenburg was said to be the best-known woman stage producer in the world.

1885-1972 ALICE GERSTENBERG

An original member of the Little Theater, Alice dramatized Alice in Wonderland *with great success.*

An original member of the Little Theater company, **Alice Gerstenberg** was a critical part of its success and important to the children's theater movement. In 1915, her dramatization of *Alice in Wonderland* was produced at Chicago's Goodman Theater and at the Booth Theater in New York, and it had long runs in both cities. The Little Theater production also toured successfully throughout the country.

A play that Alice wrote, *Overtones*, was produced in New York and Europe. This influential work was a psychological fantasy that employed an original and unusual dramatic device. It concerns two women who reveal their outer lives through the play's lines and actions, while in contrast two other veiled female characters, who represent their alter egos, express their subconscious inner characters. Eugene O'Neill used this idea later in his 1928 play *Strange Interlude*.

Outside the theater, Alice was an active clubwoman. She belonged to the Chicago Equal Suffrage Association, the Cordon Club, the Arts Club, and the Society of Midland Authors. She also founded the Playwright's Theater of Chicago.

1854-1927 CLARA LOUISE ROOT BURNHAM

Very few people know **Clara Burnham's** name, and even fewer have read her books. Her father, George F. Root, was a famous music publisher who had such songs as "The Battle Cry of Freedom" and "Tramp, Tramp, Tramp, the Boys Are Marching" on his list. Sometimes Clara wrote lyrics, and in addition she was a poet, a short story writer, and a novelist. Her novel *Sweet Clover* is considered to be a true and very complete account of the World's Columbian Exposition.

Clara wrote for women, exploring the themes that concerned them, for example the surplus of unmarried women after the Civil War or the upheaval caused as young men and women migrated from the countryside to the city. She wrote about inheritance laws and unwise investments. Her books took on subjects like suffrage, career vs. marriage, educational opportunities for women, and female independence.

She was a member of the Little Room, a place in the Fine Arts Building that celebrated conversation and attracted writers. Along with James Whitcomb Riley, Zona Gale, and Harriet Monroe, Clara founded the Society of Midland Authors.

1888-1987 FANNY AMANDA BUTCHER

While working in the Fine Arts Building as a secretary for the Little Theater, **Fanny Butcher** met Floyd Dell, the literary editor of the *Chicago Evening Post*. She pleaded with him to let her write some book reviews, and this freelance work gave her a foot in the door. She later became the longtime literary editor of the *Chicago Tribune*, but not without first working in every department of the paper in which it was possible for a woman to work. She covered fashion, beauty, society, etiquette, clubs, Sunday afternoon concerts, politics, morals court, and even a few murder trials.

Before World War I, the *Tribune* published a Saturday book page written by its chief literary critic, Elia Peattie. Fanny suggested to the Sunday editor—at the time Mary King, one of the most progressive newswomen of her day—that the Sunday edition should include some additional literary news, such as short pieces on the publishing world, notes on writers, and short reviews of best-selling books. When Mary King agreed, Fanny had a base for discussions of modern literature, as well as a way to cultivate contemporary authors.

In 1922, Fanny Butcher became the *Tribune*'s literary editor. It was the job of her dreams. As Oprah has done in a later era, Fanny could "make" a book, taking every opportunity to promote reading. For most of her own life, she read a book a day. She left the *Tribune* in 1962 after working there for fifty years.

1876-1931 RUE ANN CARPENTER

Rue Ann Carpenter traveled extensively in Europe, spoke several languages, and was an arbiter of good taste. She became the interior decorator for the Fortnightly Club, the Casino Club, a club in New York's Waldorf Hotel, and the Elizabeth Arden Salon in New York.

Chicago had shown itself to be hostile to the new twentieth century art, and so Rue Ann founded—and decorated—the Arts Club, in order to establish a forum where contemporary work could be shown and promoted. The Arts Club supported experimentation in the visual arts as well as in modern poetry, literature, music, and dance. Open to the public, the club's rooms had walls hung with the works of Georges Braque, Fernand Léger, and Pablo Picasso. Sculptures by Constantin Brancusi and Auguste Rodin were on display. Martha Graham, Bertrand Russell, Archibald MacLeish, and Edna St Vincent Millay were on the roster as guest artists, together with musicians Serge Prokofiev and Igor Stravinsky.

Rue Ann Carpenter enhanced her father's bequest of $50,000 to the Art Institute of Chicago in order to acquire works by these new artists, and she encouraged club members to contribute so that the AIC could broaden its collection.

1860-1936 HARRIET MONROE

In 1911, **Harriet Monroe** asked one hundred people to give her $50 each year so that she could publish *Poetry: A Magazine*. At the time, women entrepreneurs were few, and in any case they were frowned upon. But Harriet's magazine changed the literary culture of America forever and made Chicago a center for the encouragement of poets and poetry. Kate Buckingham, Bertha Palmer, Edith Rockefeller McCormick, and Augusta Rosenwald were among the first donors to pledge their support.

The list of those who first published their work in *Poetry* in this country is a long and notable one: there were HD (Hilda Doolittle), T. S. Eliot, D. H. Lawrence, Vachel Lindsay, Amy Lowell, Ezra Pound. Edwin Arlington Robinson, Carl Sandburg, Wallace Stevens, Sara Teasdale, William Carlos Williams, and W. B. Yeats among the contributors.

In addition, Harriet edited poetry anthologies in 1917, 1925, 1932, and 1936. Entitled *The New Poetry*, these addressed new audiences, especially students.

1851–1936   ANNA MORGAN

Sarah Siddons was one of the leading British actors of her day when **Anna Morgan**, who had performed as a monologuist in and around Chicago, persuaded Siddons to let her become part of her program. This success in turn convinced a theatrical agency to accept her as a client, and the agency booked her into theaters in New York, Boston, and some cities in the Midwest.

Anna's monologues ranged from homespun yarns to pieces by Browning, Shakespeare, Schiller, and Christina Rossetti. On stage she was relaxed, telling a story in a natural, comfortable way rather than emoting with great drama. It was unique for the time and won her appreciative audiences.

The Chicago Opera House Conservatory (later the Chicago Conservatory) asked her to teach drama, and this soon became her main occupation. In 1899 she was the first to stage a George Bernard Shaw play, *Candida*, in America. Then, in 1902, she shocked Shaw when her American premiere of *Caesar and Cleopatra* boasted a cast composed only of women.

Anna opened a studio and school in the Fine Arts Building in 1890. The suite of eight rooms not only had a stage but also a well-equipped gym, because her training stressed good health, physical grace, and mental well-being. Later she added deportment, stagecraft, French, and dramatic literature to the curriculum. Her school was a training ground for professional actors and teachers.

SIDE TRIP

It is worth going into the venerable old Fine Arts Building, which continues to house architects, musicians, artists, and not-for-profit arts groups. You might go up to the tenth floor, where two walls are decorated with murals by J. C. Leyendecker. You can quietly explore the hallways and then walk down. The previous owner put up a series of small plaques near most doorways to identify the locations of the Little Theater, Anna Morgan's studio, the Poetry office, and other notable tenants. On the first floor you will find two theaters. The smaller one, the World Playhouse, often saw productions by the Playwrights Theater of Chicago from 1922 through 1945.

1863-1952 BERTHA VAN HOOSEN

As you leave the Fine Arts Building by its south door, you will see a plaque commemorating **Bertha Van Hoosen**, who earned an M.D. in 1888 and opened a practice in Chicago in 1892. Bertha was on call as an emergency doctor during the Columbian Exposition, but she found it very difficult to build a practice. She was also trained as a surgeon, but the Chicago Hospital for Women and Children (renamed for Mary Harris Thompson; see Tour I) was the only hospital in the city where she was allowed to operate. In 1899, Provident Hospital opened to serve a biracial community, and Van Hoosen was accredited there. She brought a considerable number of white patients to the hospital; in the early years that was a critical factor in its survival.

Dr. Van Hoosen gave sex education and sexual anatomy lectures and classes to many different groups of women—clubwomen, mothers and children, working girls, and high school girls. Although she was successful, she faced many hurdles during her career. One success was that she trained twenty women as surgeons who otherwise had few options. Medical schools and hospitals designated for women only were gradually giving way to integrated institutions, but the transition was slow and difficult.

 Next door to the Fine Arts Building is Roosevelt University, named after Eleanor and Franklin D. Roosevelt.

1930-1965 LORRAINE VIVIAN HANSBERRY

Originally known as Roosevelt College, the school opened shortly after World War II, a time when most institutions of higher education in the United States either excluded Jews or had a quota system. African-Americans were even more likely to be excluded, or else admitted in very small numbers. Roosevelt College was dedicated to open enrollment.

The playwright **Lorraine Hansberry** attended Roosevelt for a short time. She was born in Chicago, and in her memoir she castigated Chicago public schools for "withholding" education from African-American children.

The important play Lorraine wrote, *A Raisin in the Sun*, had successful tryouts in several cities, including Chicago, before it went on to a stunningly successful New York run that began in 1959. Lorraine won the New York Drama Critics Circle award that year, the youngest person to do so, and the first African-American.

A major American playwright, Lorraine had a brilliant career that was cut short by cancer. She died in 1963 at the age of thirty-four.

Chicago now has twenty-four parks named for women. Lucy Parsons, Mahalia Jackson, Lucy Flower, Chi Che Wang, and Bessie Coleman are some of those so honored. Lorraine Hansberry is another. The park named for her is located at 5635 South Indiana Avenue.

1904-1964 ROSE HUM LEE

Born in Montana, **Rose Hum** attended grammar and high school there. After marrying in the late 1920s, she and her husband went to China and were there when the struggle began between the Chinese Communist Party and Chiang Kai-shek's Kuomintang National Party (KMT) for control of China. The KMT was also engaged in a huge effort to resist invasion by the Japanese. Rose supported these efforts and was in Canton during eighteen months of continual bombing of the area by the Japanese. She volunteered her time to work with refugees and war orphans.

Rose returned to the United States in 1938 with an adopted daughter, a war orphan. Although other relatives objected, Rose's mother supported her daughter's return to school to get a college degree by taking care of the little girl. Rose entered the University of Chicago to study sociology. When she received her Ph.D. in 1947, she was already teaching in the sociology department at what was then Roosevelt College.

Eventually Rose became the chair of the department, the first Chinese-American to chair an academic department at an American university. As a sociologist, her research centered on Chinese immigrants and citizens in the United States; she was the only person to study this minority group for the next twenty years. In 1960, her book *The Chinese in the United States of America* brought together all of the findings of her research on Chinese-American communities throughout the country.

SIDE TRIP

The Roosevelt University building was designed by the architectural firm of Louis Sullivan and Dankmar Adler and is a wonderful early example of a multipurpose building. The main entrance on Michigan Avenue led into what was the Auditorium Hotel. If you step back or cross the street, you will be able to see a seventeen-story tower above the former hotel that housed offices, including the Sullivan & Adler firm on the top floor. On the Congress Street side of the building, an entrance led to the third part of the building, the Auditorium Theater.

Completed in 1889, the Auditorium Hotel was the finest in the city. Unfortunately, it was built just a few years before patrons of exclusive hotels began to demand private bathrooms. The luxury hotel suddenly became out-of-date and old-fashioned. During the depression it went bankrupt, and it stood empty until World War II, when it was turned into a USO Club. After the war, it began a new life as a school.

Enter the building, and you will find a beautiful mosaic and marble lobby and a reception desk. Climb the wide steps to the second floor and walk straight ahead. You will be in part of the former hotel's sitting room, facing Michigan Avenue with wonderful views of Buckingham Fountain. Just to your left is the Sullivan Room, on the Congress Street side. Beautifully restored, it is now used for receptions. It is not always open, but you might ask at the reception desk on the first floor if you can see it.

Another room that is not always open to view is Ganz Hall on the seventh floor. When it was used as a sleeping room for officers during World War II, the stained glass windows were obscured with paint. It has been restored and is now used for concerts, many of which are free; you may want to ask for a concert schedule or get on the mailing list. This beautiful hall has a low-ceilinged outer lobby designed by Frank Lloyd Wright, an apprentice to Sullivan at the time.

Not to be missed is the tenth floor library. Originally it was the hotel dining room, with a wonderful skylight and the best-looking radiator covers in the entire city.

Walk around the corner on Congress Street to the Auditorium Theater.

This 4,200-seat theater is one of the most beautiful in the world, and it has superb acoustics. When Adelina Patti sang on opening night in 1889, it was truly a glittering affair, in part because it was one of the first theaters to use electric lights.

The theater was built for opera, and the Chicago Opera Company quickly became a tenant. So did the Chicago Symphony Orchestra, although it moved out and into its own building in 1901. Then in 1929 the Civic Opera House was built on the west side of the downtown area. It was the beginning of the Great Depression, and, along with the Auditorium Hotel, the lights went out in the Auditorium Theater. Servicemen used the huge stage as a bowling alley during World War II.

After Roosevelt College opened in 1945, it operated on a shoestring for a number of years, with little money for restoration and certainly no funds to reopen the theater. Still, many Chicagoans could fondly remember magical performances, perhaps with actor Sarah Bernhardt or ballerina Anna Pavlova.

Fortunately, as the years passed the notion of architectural preservation came into prominence. Chicago had already lost two

SIDE TRIP

East of Michigan is Buckingham Fountain, at Congress and Columbus streets. There is a story that friends urged Kate Buckingham to go to the most exclusive hat maker in Chicago; at the time women were wearing elaborate hats adorned with feathers and fruits and flowers. Kate looked around, chose a very simple hat, and asked the price. "Fifty dollars," the salesperson replied. "Fifty dollars!" exclaimed Kate. "My dear, I can't afford fifty dollars; I'm building a fountain!" The fountain cost $750,000 and began its sparkling display on August 26, 1927. A band conducted by John Phillip Sousa played a composition called "Water Sprites." The huge crowd eagerly anticipated the rush of water; when a switch turned it on, blue lights illuminated the splashing cascade. In typical Kate Buckingham fashion, the fountain was dedicated to her brother, Clarence.

Sullivan masterpieces: the Garrick Theater had been torn down to make way for a parking lot, and the Chicago Stock Exchange building had been reduced to rubble. In the 1950s, an Independent Auditorium Theater Council was organized, a volunteer group chaired by a dedicated and determined woman, Beatrice Spachner. The council raised the $3 million that was needed, and the theater triumphantly re-opened in 1967.

See a performance at the Auditorium Theater if you can. If architecture is sometimes defined as frozen music, this space, from the lobby to the rooftop, is an unforgettable hymn. Tours are sometimes given; call the theater for times and fees.

The Art Institute saved and restored part of Sullivan's Stock Exchange building, the trading room. You can see it on the first floor of AIC on the Columbus Avenue side.

1893-1963 ROSA BURSCHSTEIN RAISA

Chicagoans began to attend and appreciate opera from the 1850s on. At first, the opportunity to see an opera came only when a traveling opera company visited the city. In the 1890s there was a great rush to establish resident cultural institutions and, after the Chicago Symphony Orchestra was founded, demand increased for a resident opera company.

A refugee from a 1907 Russian pogrom, **Rosa Raisa** fled to Italy and studied voice on the isle of Capri. When Chicago's first resident company, the Chicago Grand Opera Company, was formed in 1909, Rosa became a member of the fledgling group. In 1913 she made her debut as a prima donna at the Auditorium Theater, in Verdi's *Aida*.

Despite this triumph, at the end of the season the Chicago company was out of funds. Rosa began a world tour and established an international reputation. Three years later, she returned to a reorganized Chicago Opera Association. She had a brilliant voice and sang lead roles with the company for sixteen successive seasons.

Rosa was one of the first operatic sopranos to make recordings, beginning in 1917 and continuing through 1933. With the Chicago Opera Association she sang *Aida* for the first time on radio in 1922. It was performed in its entirety on Chicago's WYW radio station.

After she retired from the stage, Rosa had a studio in the Fine Arts Building, where she taught through the 1950s. She also served as an advisor to the founders of the Lyric Opera Company.

1874-1967 MARY GARDEN

"Our Own" was the way Chicagoans spoke of **Mary Garden**. Born in Scotland, Mary moved with her family in 1887, at the age of thirteen, to the south-side neighborhood of Hyde Park, then a Chicago suburb. She subsequently studied voice with Sarah Robinson Duff, who encouraged her students by finding paying engagements for them in local clubs and theaters or by giving recitals in private homes. Duff also took them to operas and plays. Mary soon dropped out of Hyde Park High School to study music full-time.

Duff recognized Mary's talent and encouraged her to continue her vocal studies in Europe. The Garden family could not afford this, so Duff persuaded another pupil, a very wealthy woman, to finance the project. She herself then accompanied Mary as chaperone when Mary went to Paris in 1896. After Duff returned home, Mary boarded with a Parisian family so that she could perfect her French and concentrate on her music.

After three years, her Chicago sponsor let her know that she would no longer provide funds. An American soprano, Sybil Sanderson, befriended her, and Mary lived in a room in Sanderson's apartment. More importantly, Sanderson gave her an opportunity to meet Albert Carré, the director of the Opéra-Comique, who invited Mary to

> Her dance of the seven veils in *Salome* made "Our Own" famous—if not notorious.

SIDE TRIP

The main branch of the Chicago Public Library is located in its new building one block west of the Auditorium Theater, at State and Congress. Aside from numerous public programs and special exhibits, the library displays more than eighty works of art, many by local artists. Some works deal specifically with Chicago history, such as the terrazzo and inlaid brass piece entitled **DuSable's Journey** *on the lower level or several bronze busts by Lorado Taft on the ninth floor in the Special Collections Reading Room. About one-fourth of the art is by women. There is a bust of Gwendolyn Brooks done by Sara Miller on the seventh floor and a wonderful wall hanging on the fifth floor by Claire Zeisler, entitled* **Madagascar V**. *A pamphlet is available at the information desk on the first floor, as are monthly event calendars.*

come to rehearsals. Soon after, she was hired as an understudy, and she thus gained a meager but sustaining income.

The dream of every aspiring young singer or actor came true for Mary in 1900 when the star of Charpentier's opera *Louise* became ill during a performance. Mary was called upon to sing the title role in the third act and was, of course, an "instant sensation." Building upon her lucky break, she became very well known in Europe, developing a unique style in which she fused her vocal powers with a talent for dramatization and used costumes and stagecraft to enhance her roles and make them memorable.

In 1907, Mary returned to the United States to become a star in the newly organized Manhattan Opera Company. American audiences knew very little about French opera, and she worried about the reception these operas would receive. She persuaded the New York group to import entire productions, including all the cast members, from the Opéra-Comique, a public relations coup that stimulated audience anticipation and opened an entirely new era of opera in the United States.

In 1910, Mary Garden reappeared in her hometown. Harold and Edith Rockefeller McCormick had organized a group of Chicagoans with deep pockets who bought the Manhattan Opera Company, transported it to Chicago, and renamed it the Chicago Grand Opera Company. Mary's first role for the new Chicago company was in Debussy's *Pélleas et Mélisande*. Later in the same season, she took on the role that made her famous—if not notorious. It was the opera *Salome*, in which she performed the dance of the seven veils. The Chicago Law and Order League managed to get the opera off the stage after only two performances.

Mary was now Chicago's prima donna, and she remained so for the next two decades. She championed new music and also became a cultural ambassador for Chicago, singing in more than

1,225 performances on tour with the Chicago Grand Opera Company and in countless solo concerts. She was dubbed "Mary the First" when she became director of the company during the 1921–1922 season—and an exciting season it was. She gave eighteen performances that year, including *Salome*; she revived Puccini's *Girl of the Golden West* for Rosa Raisa; and she gave Chicagoans an opportunity to hear Richard Wagner's operas sung in German after they had been driven out of the repertoire by anti-German sentiment during and after World War I. The world premiere of Sergey Prokofiev's *The Love for Three Oranges* had a very lavish production.

All this artistic success was achieved by very nearly bankrupting the company, and Mary stepped down when the season ended in 1922. She continued singing with the Chicago company until 1931 and in Paris until 1934. After she retired, she gave master classes and signed on as a musical advisor and talent scout for the MGM movie company.

This is the end of Tour III.

FOR FURTHER READING

Potawatomi Indians

James A. Clifton, *The Potawatomi, Indians of North America Series* (New York, NY: Chelsea House Publishers, 1987). This is a readable, concise introduction to the history of the tribe; for a more scholarly treatment, see below.

James A. Clifton, *The Prairie People: Continuity and Change in Potawatomi Indian Culture* 1665–1965 (Lawrence, KS: The Regents Press of Kansas, 1977).

Métis

This French word meaning "of mixed blood" was used to describe the children of Native American mothers and European fathers.

Jennifer S. H. Brown, *Strangers in Blood: Fur Trade Company Families in Indian Country* (Vancouver, BC: University of British Columbia Press, 1980).

Sylvia Van Kirk, *Many Tender Ties: Women in the Fur Trade Society* (Norman, OK: University of Oklahoma Press; 1980). Although both Brown's and this book are scholarly, the Van Kirk book is the more readable of the two.

Early Chicago History

Juliette Augusta McGill Kinzie, *Wau-Bun: The "Early Days" in the Northwest* (Chicago, IL: D. B. Crocket and Company, 1856). As a daughter-in-law of Eleanor Lytle McKillop and John Kinzie, Juliette puts a spin on the importance of her husband's family to the founding of Chicago. Nevertheless, this is a very useful book for the oral-history story of Eleanor's capture and for the many details of domestic and early village life. Recently reprinted by the Michigan Historical Society.

An Early Chicago History web site is: www.earlychicagohistory.com

Chicago Women's History

Rima Lumin Schultz and Adele Hast et al, eds., *Women Building Chicago 1790–1990: A Biographical Dictionary* (Bloomington, IN: Indiana University Press, 2001). The definitive reference book for the history of Chicago women, it is available from the Chicago Area Women's History Council website, www.cawhc.org.

Marilyn A. Domer, Jean S. Hunt, Mary Ann Johnson, and Adade M Wheeler, *Walking With Women through Chicago History: Four Self-Guided Tours* (Chicago, IL: Salsedo Press, 1981). This small book (also available at www.cawhc.org) resulted from several very successful women's history bus tours sponsored by the Chicago Area Women's History Council. It covers four areas of the city: Prairie Avenue, Hyde Park, Hull House and the West Side, and the Loop. Some references to sites and to suggested restaurants may be outdated.

Indeed, in the two years that I have been working on ***Walking With Women II***, I have been surprised at how often I have had to update material. Plaques disappear, buildings get torn down, statues are put in storage, and a dynamic city keeps changing, Nevertheless, the original book, as well as this one, remind you of women already known to you and tell of others of whom you may never have heard. All of their stories are well worth reading.

INDEX

A

Abbott, Merriel, 60-61
  See also
  Palmer House Hotel
Abercrombie, Gertrude, 83
Addams, Jane, 49, 100
Alpiner, Molly.
  See Molly Newbury
Alsop, Marin, 97
Anderson, Margaret, 102-03
Anderson, Mary, 52
Anthony, Susan B., 64, 78
Antiquarian Society, 93-94
Art Institute of Chicago, 23, 59, 74, 76-77, 79, 80, 82-83, 85, 87, 90-94, 99, 106, 112
  See also
  School of the Art Institute
Auditorium Hotel, 110-11
Auditorium Theater, 94, 110-12, 114

B

Baker, Edna, 73
Bauer, Sybil, 21
Bennett, Bessie, 93-94
Big White Man, 11-13
Black Partridge, 17
Blackshear, Kathleen, 81-82
Bond, Carrie Jacobs, 42
Boston Store, The, 61-62
Bowen, Louise DeKoven, 100
Bradwell, Myra Colby, 33, 77
Brod, Fritzi Schermer, 30
Browne, Ellen Von Volkenburg, 103

Buckingham, Kate Sturgis, 92, 106, 110-11
Buckingham Fountain, 92, 110-11
Burnham, Clara Root, 104-05
Burnham, Daniel, 86
  Burnham & Root
  (architects), 80
Butcher, Fanny, 105

C

Carpenter, Rue Ann, 105-06
Carse, Matilda, 55-56
Carson Pirie Scott & Co., 65-67
Cassatt, Mary, 75, 82, 90
Cassidy, Claudia, 35
Century of Progress, A. See
  World's Fair of 1933
Chappell, Eliza. See Eliza Porter
Chicago Cultural Center, 4, 33-36
Chicago Exposition Building, 75
Chicago fire of 1871, 19, 37, 39, 41, 49, 74, 80
Chicago Historical Society/
  Chicago History Museum, 84, 99
Chicago Hospital for Women and Children, 48-49, 63, 108
Chicago Public Library, 34-35, 114
Chicago River, 2-3, 8, 19-21
Chicago Symphony Orchestra, 94-96, 98, 111-12
  Chorus of, 96-97
Chicago Teachers Federation/
  Union, 32

Chicago Temple, the, 44, 46-47
Chicago Tourism Center, 34
Chicago Tribune, the, 30, 35, 97, 105
Chicago Tribute markers, 4, 34
Chicago Women's Hospital.
  See Chicago Hospital
  for Women and Children
Chorpenning, Charlotte, 24
Cicely, a slave, 14, 16
Colburn, Annie, 92-93
Columbian Exposition. See
  World's Columbian
  Exposition of 1893
Congress of Representative
  Women. See World's
  Columbian Exposition
  of 1893
Crouse, Rumah, 72

D

Dagenais, Margaret Marie, 86
Daley, Eleanor "Sis", 35
Daley Center, 27, 48
Darrow, Clarence, 46, 103
Depression, the Great, 25, 32, 62, 66, 73
Doggett, Kate Newell, 100-01
Dreier, Margaret. See
  Margaret Robins
Du Sable. Catherine, 3-4, 6-7
Du Sable, Jean Baptiste
  Point, 3-4, 6, 114

E

Empire Room. *See* Palmer House Hotel

Equal Rights Amendment, 46
See also Women's suffrage movement

F

Fenberg, Matilda, 46

Field, Florence Lathrop, 79

Field's. *See* Marshall Field's

Fine Arts Building (Michigan Avenue), 98-99, 101, 103, 105, 107-08, 113

Fine Arts Building (World's Fair). *See* World's Columbian Exposition of 1893

Fort Dearborn, 8-10, 13-18
Massacre, 15-17, 19

Fortnightly Club, 58, 99-101, 105

Fountain of the Great Lakes, 90

Foy, Frances, 85

Freer, Eleanor, 42

Fur trade, 4-5, 7

G

Gaines, Irene McCoy, 53-54

Garden, Mary, 113-15

Gardner, Helen, 81-82

Garrett, Eliza Clark, 44-45

Geraghty, Helen Tieken, 25

Gerstenberg, Alice, 104

Glover, Jane, 98

Glove Workers union, 51-52

Goggin, Catherine, 31-32

Goodman Theater, 23-26, 38, 41, 104
School of Drama, 24-25

Great Fire, the.
See Chicago fire of 1871

Grimm, Edith Rambar, 66

Gscheidle, Gertrude, 34

Gustafson, Kathryn, 36

H

Haley, Margaret, 31-32

Hallowell, Sara Tyson, 75-76

Hansberry, Lorraine, 108-09

Harris Theater for Music and Dance, Joan W. and Irving R., 36

Harrison, Elizabeth, 72-73

Harshaw, Ruth Hetzel, 66-67

Hart, Pearl, 47

Haskins, Sylvia Shaw Judson, 27

Hayden, Sophia, 58

Heald, Nathan, 14-17

Heald, Rebekah Wells, 14-17

Heald Square monument, 90

Heap, Jane, 102-03

Hedger, Caroline, 67-68

Helm, Margaret McKillop, 17

Henrotin, Ellen, 77-78

Hetzel, Ruth. *See* Ruth Harshaw

Hillis, Margaret, 96-97

Hoge, Jane, 22, 48, 63-65

Holt, Nora, 95

Hull House, 25, 47, 49-50, 100

Hum, Rose. *See* Rose Lee

I

Illinois Central Railroad, 37-38

J

Joliet, Louis, 3, 19

Judson, Sylvia Shaw.
See Sylvia Haskins

K

Kemeys, Edward and Laura, 79

Kinzie, Eleanor "Nelly" Lytle McKillop, 10-13

Kinzie, John, 10, 13-16, 19

Kinzie, John Harris, 10

Kinzie, Juliette McGill, 10-12

Kinzie, Margaret (first wife of John), 10, 13

L

La Lime, Jean, 8, 10

Lee, Rose Hum, 109

Little Review, the, 102-03

Little Room, 105

Little Theater, 102-05, 107

Livermore, Mary, 22, 33, 48, 63-65

Lytle, Eleanor.
See Eleanor Kinzie

M

MacMonnies, Mary Fairchild, 76

Macy's (department store), 28, 61

Marquette, Jacques, 3, 19

Marshall Field's (department store), 28-31, 61

McCormick, Cyrus, 20

McCormick, Edith Rockefeller, 106, 114

McCormick, Harold, 114

McCormick, Nancy "Nettie" Fowler, 20

McCormick, Ruth, 31, 53

McCormick Reaper Works, 20

McCoy, Irene. *See* Irene Gaines

McDowell, Mary, 49

Mercy Hospital, 69

Métis ("mixed blood"), 5, 17

Millennium Park, 36, 38, 41
  Cloud Gate, 36
  Crown Fountain, 36
  Lurie Garden, 36
  Pritzker Pavilion, 36
Monholland, Mother Mary Francis DeSales, 70-71
Monroe, Harriet, 103, 105-06
Moody, Harriet Converse Tilden, 29
Morgan, Anna, 107

N

National Association of Colored Women's Clubs, the, 53
National Lawyers Guild, the, 47
National College of Education/National Louis University, 71-73
Netcher, Molly. *See* Molly Newbury
Nestor, Agnes, 51-52
Nevelson, Louise, 36, 57
Newbury, Molly Alpiner Netcher, 62
Northwest Ordinance, 14
Northwestern Sanitary Commission, 63-64

O

O'Brien, Mother Mary Agatha, 68-69
O'Leary, Catherine and Patrick, 40
  Cow of, 40
Orchestra Hall, 94-97
Ouilmette, Antoine,, 5-8, 17-18
Ouilmette, Archange, 5-7, 17-18

P

Page, Lucy, 57-58
Palmer, Bertha Honore, 58-59, 75-76, 91, 106
Palmer, Pauline Lennards, 82
Palmer, Potter, 58-59
Palmer House (Hilton) Hotel, 58, 60-61
  Empire Room of, 60
Peterson, Anna, 29-30
Platt, Ida, 63
Poetry magazine, 106-07
Point du Sable. *See* Du Sable
Porter, Eliza Chappell, 21-22
Potawatomi Indians, 3-5, 15, 18
Potter, Bessie. *See* Bessie Vonnoh
Price, Florence, 42, 95-96
Provident Hospital, 78, 108

R

Raisa, Rosa, 112-13, 115
Ran, Shulamit, 98
Robins, Margaret Dreier, 50-51
Romanoff, Maya, 36
Roosevelt College/University, 108-11
Rosenwald, Augusta, 106
Rudolph, Anne, 41

S

Schermer, Fritzi. *See* Fritzi Brod
School of the Art Institute, 19, 36, 38, 79-83, 85-87, 89, 93-94, 98, 102
Seaton, Irene. *See* Irene Wicker
Seneca Indians, 10-13
Shaw, Annie, 82
Sisters of Mercy, 68-71
Spachner, Beatrice, 112
Sprague, Nancy, 90
Stevenson, Sarah Hackett, 77, 87
Stone, Lucy, 33, 64
Sullivan, Louis, 71, 110, 111-12
  Sullivan & Adler company, 110
Sundstrom, Ebba, 42-43

T

Taft, Lorado, 86-90, 99, 114
Theater District, 23-24
Thomas, Augusta Reed, 98
Thompson, Mary Harris, 22, 48-49, 108
Tieken, Helen. *See* Helen Geraghty
Tiffany, Louis Comfort, 23, 34
Tilden, Harriet Converse. *See* Harriet Moody
Torrey, Mabel Landrum, 89
Treaty of Paris, 7

U

United States Sanitary Commission, 48, 63-64

V

Van Hoosen, Bertha, 108
Van Pappelendam, Laura, 80
Vonnoh, Bessie, 87-88

W

Walker, Nellie, 89-90
Wau Bun, 10, 12
Weisberg, Lois, 36
Welge, Gladys, 43
Wells, Billy, 14, 16
Wells, Clara Barak, 98-99
Wells, Rebekah.
   See Rebekah Heald
Wells, Sarajane, 83-84
Wendt, Julia Bracken, 86-87
Whistler, Ann Bishop, 8-10
Whistler, George Washington, 9
Whistler, James McNeill, 9
Whistler, John, 8-9, 13-14
Whistler, Julia Fearson, 8-9
Whistler, Sarah, 9
Whistler, William, 8-9
Wicker, Irene Seaton, 25-27
Willard, Frances, 55-57, 77
Williams, Fannie Barrier, 78
Wilmette (Illinois town).
   See Ouilmette
Women's Christian Temperance Union, 54-57
Women's suffrage movement, 46, 64, 78, 99-100, 101, 104
Women's Symphony Orchestra of Chicago, 42-43, 96
Women's Temple, 54, 56-57
Women's Trade Union League, 31, 49-50, 52-53

World's Columbian Exposition of 1893, 58-59, 75-77, 79-80, 82, 86-89, 92, 104, 108
   Board of Lady Managers, 58-59
   Congress of Representative Women, 59, 76-78
   Fine Arts Building (at the fair), 59, 76, 82, 88
   Woman's Building, 58-59, 75-77, 88
World's Fair of 1933, 25, 96
Wright, Frank Lloyd, 110

X

Xavier Academy, 69-70

Printed in the United States
78119LV00006B/1-15